Life's a Pitch...

How to sell yourself and your brilliant ideas

Stephen Bayley, BY ROGER MAVITY

When I first met Stephen and he was introduced to me as an academic, an art historian and an author, I feared he might prove a little too earnest for my taste. But then he gave me a copy of his latest book: it was not entitled *Post-structuralism Reassessed* but *Sex, Drink and Fast Cars* and I realized that we had more in common than I had expected.

As I got to know Stephen better, I discovered that he wasn't only interested in sex, drink and fast cars: he is also interested in tennis. (But you can only play tennis in the summer, whereas the other three sports are year-round activities.)

In much the same way as marriage is widely held to be the best way of spoiling a good romance, so working together is often the best way of spoiling a good friendship. That hasn't proved to be the case with Stephen and me. We were good friends long before we conceived the idea of this book, but working together has cemented that friendship. I've learnt that Stephen has, beneath the surface, an encyclopaedic knowledge and a penetrating intelligence, while on the surface he has great style and a mischievous sense of fun – not a bad formula for enjoying life, if you think about it.

In between books and broadcasting, Stephen has found time to be the first head of the Design Museum and a consultant on design strategy to such huge corporations as Coca-Cola and the Ford Motor Company.

People often tell us that they're surprised we're good friends, because we're so different. What are they trying to say – that I *don't* like sex, drink and fast cars?

ON STEPHEN BAYLEY:
'I don't know anybody with more interesting ideas about style, taste and contemporary design.' *Tom Wolfe*

Roger Mavity, BY STEPHEN BAYLEY

'What time of day is it, Rog?' In the familiar joke about
the moral bankruptcy of the advertising business, Rog
would reply, 'What time of day would you like it to be?'
But while Roger Mavity has many of the Machiavellian
talents and predispositions required to get to the very top
of a business that George Orwell likened to the 'rattling
of a stick in a swill bucket', he is wholly without the
supine reflexes of advertising's groundlings. On the
contrary, Rog gives a clear impression of being very much
in charge. All that time in the swill bucket was not wasted.

Before we met, he had an apprenticeship at an agency
called French Gold Abbott that matured (if, that is,
anything in adland ever actually improves with age) into
the best of the best. Rog was there when the Habitat and
Volvo accounts were pitched for, won and executed with
a superior intelligence and style that raised the game in
British advertising. But if business is a battle, no one
knows better than Rog that it is a bit like Stendhal's
account of Waterloo: foggy chaos interrupted by
sporadic bouts of furious activity.

He has built and sold his own agency. Working for
Granada, he ran the successful pitch for Forte Group, the
biggest and most bitter takeover battle the London Stock
Exchange has ever seen. While I was once director of one
of Terence Conran's far-flung dominions, Rog became
chief executive of the whole Conran empire. He has thus
acquired the authority of an infinitely wise, if sometimes
sardonic, media Buddha. He takes photographs, he sails.
He talks. In fact, his wife says he 'talks in paragraphs'.
This is his first and, he says, his last book. A pity, because
I have never enjoyed any collaboration so much.

ON ROGER MAVITY:
'Without doubt, the best presenter I have ever met.'
Charles Allen, founding Chief Executive of ITV

Life's a Pitch ...

How to sell yourself
and your brilliant ideas

**Stephen Bayley
& Roger Mavity**

CORGI BOOKS

TRANSWORLD PUBLISHERS
61–63 Uxbridge Road, London W5 5SA
www.penguin.co.uk

Transworld is part of the Penguin Random House group of companies
whose addresses can be found at global.penguinrandomhouse.com

Penguin
Random House
UK

First published in Great Britain in 2007 by Bantam Press
an imprint of Transworld Publishers
Corgi edition published 2008
Corgi edition reissued 2017

A CIP catalogue record for this book
is available from the British Library.

ISBN
9780552174862

Typeset in Din Regular 10/13pt
Printed and bound by Clays Ltd, Elcograf S.p.A.

Penguin Random House is committed to a sustainable
future for our business, our readers and our planet. This book
is made from Forest Stewardship Council® certified paper.

MIX
Paper from
responsible sources
FSC® C018179

3 5 7 9 10 8 6 4

This book is dedicated to
Niccolò Machiavelli,
whose ruthless understanding
of personal ambition has
inspired us both.

Pitch (pit-*sch*), v. [ME. *Piche(n; also later pitched)*. Origin, history and sense-development are obsc.].

1. To thrust in, fix in; make fast, settle, set, place. **2.** To plant, implant; to fix, stick, fasten. Later to make fast with stakes. **3.** To place or locate oneself; to take up position, settle or alight. **4.** To set in order, arrange; to fix the order, position, rate, price or value of. **5.** To pit (one person) *against* another. **6.** To fix, settle, or place in thought. **7.** To present, strut, flog, blag, persuade *in order* to win a deal.

Con

Book One

Book Two

Appendix

How to use

Making a pitch is not just a matter of winning the pet-food account in an airless meeting room at one of those hotels where people conduct that sort of business. The whole of life is a pitch. Everything you do is a matter of presentation and persuasion. Getting dressed. Dating. Lunch. Sending an e-mail. As soon as you get the idea, it becomes infectious. But, until now, there has never been an inspirational book written on the subject of how to do it.

Stephen Bayley and Roger Mavity have similar philosophies, but from very different backgrounds. Unsurprisingly perhaps, they have chosen to write two different books on the same subject in the same cover. Roger wrote the first book and Stephen wrote the second, although they have been continuously interfering in each other's territory. The result is both a business manual and a philosophy for life.

In the first book Roger looks at pitching in a highly pragmatic way: how do you design and deliver your pitch to get the result you want? He examines how you pitch in business and how you can do it far

this book

better. He goes on to look at the parallels between the way you pitch for business and the way you pitch yourself in life. You can use Roger's part of the book to understand the mechanics (as well as the psychology) of a brilliant pitch and to learn how to do it yourself.

Stephen's book is more discursive and anecdotal. Intended to be provocative, it looks at the differences between appearance and reality, between style and substance, between who you are and what you want to be and how bad behaviour can sometimes get good results. Whether discussing business or life, this is in a way the ultimate design book because it is a book about how to design your personality.

Although **Life's a Pitch ...** is in two distinct parts, there's a single large idea behind the book. How you pitch your ideas and how you pitch yourself will determine the course of your life. Learning how to do it effectively (and understanding why you need to) can mean the difference between success and failure: because the truth is that **the whole of life's a pitch ...**

Book
1

1 Why it matters

Life is not a pattern of gradually evolving improvement. It's a series of long, fallow patches punctuated by moments of crucial change. How you handle the long fallow stretches doesn't matter much. How you handle the moments of change is vital.

THAT'S TRUE in business: the moment of crucial change may be an interview for a new job; the board agreeing (or failing to agree) your plans for the coming year; a presentation to win a big new project. It's these moments when you're pitching for a step-change that things really matter.

The same is true in life as in business. It's the chance encounter which becomes a new friendship. It's persuading the bank to lend you the money to buy the house you've always dreamt of. It's the evening date which, handled right, becomes a passionate affair.

These big moments are not decided by chance – they're decided by how you handle them. How you pitch your case is what makes the difference.

The pitch is the hinge on which the door opens. Everything else in life is about process – the pitch is about decisions: the decision to give you the funds to start your own business; the decision to marry. If you get the pitch right, everything follows. And if you don't, nothing follows.

This book is not dedicated to the 98 per cent of our lives spent on the banal gaps between the big pitch moments. It's dedicated to that 2 per cent of pitch moments which really decide the success or failure of the whole 100 per cent.

2 It's theatre, not information

The pitch moments, those crucial moments which give the opportunity for big change, all have one thing in common. You are trying to get someone else to do what you want them to do – to hire you, to sleep with you, to lend you a million pounds to start your own business . . .

PEOPLE ALWAYS assume that the key to these moments of persuasion is to present the information which should make people change their minds (here's the logical reason why you should lend me a million pounds . . .) but actually these encounters depend much less on logic and much more on emotion than people think.

Someone being asked to lend a million pounds is faced really with only one simple question to answer: will I get my money back? And of course that isn't a logical question, because it's asking to know the future. There is no logic which can describe what is going to happen a few years from now.

Yet while you can't know what's going to happen, you can think you know. Indeed a banker who spends his whole life lending money is endlessly 'deciding' what will happen in the future. But, of course, he is not deciding, he is just guessing. He will never call it a guess – that's too scarily truthful. He'll call it an 'informed estimate', an 'intelligent assumption', a 'considered opinion'. But believe me, it's a guess. No one can foretell the future.

A banker doesn't know whether he'll get his money back; a date doesn't know whether what lies ahead is three hours of tedium or thirty years of partnership.

So when you're pitching to someone, you're asking them to judge the future. Since knowing the future is beyond logic, their judgement won't be based on logical factors but on emotional factors: trust, confidence, hope, ambition, desire.

These factors aren't rational, they are instinctive. They are not of the head, they are of the heart.

Of course, logical arguments and rational thought have an important part to play in a successful pitch, because they can underpin emotional instinct with reassurance. But logic in a pitch is never an end in itself, it's only a means to an end.

So to pitch successfully, you have to understand that it's not about widening someone's knowledge base, it's about giving them a jolting power surge to their emotional electricity.

A pitch does not take place in the library of the mind, it takes place in the theatre of the heart.

3 Think 'playwright', not 'actor'

It's easy to be mesmerized by a presenter who's good on his feet into thinking that good presentation is all about good delivery – if I put it across well, then it's a good pitch.

NOTHING COULD be further from the truth. If the content isn't strong no amount of polished delivery will save it. If Kenneth Branagh plays a brilliant Hamlet, we can all admire Branagh's acting skill – but we still know that it's Shakespeare who wrote the play. And no actor was ever remembered for a great performance in a bad play. That's why actors all yearn to play the great roles – they know that they can only do great work with great raw material.

So, when you set about a pitch, don't think *actor* (how well can I deliver this?) but think *playwright* (how well can I write this?). A great performance starts with a great script.

Sir Gerry Robinson had a characteristically pithy insight into this issue. Gerry started life as the ninth of ten children born to a poor Donegal carpenter and went on to become the chairman of not one but two FTSE 100 companies, Chairman of the Arts Council and a multi-millionaire in his own right, so his views on the workplace are worth listening to. In a large meeting, one of his colleagues was described as a good presenter. Gerry looked witheringly and said, 'There's no such thing as a good presenter.' Then he added, 'There's only a clear thinker.'

Gerry's point was simple but fundamental. A presenter, however good his delivery, is only as good as the presentation he is delivering. And if the train of thought in the presentation is clear, then the delivery will inevitably seem clear too.

Gerry is right. People do talk about good presenters in the same way they talk about good actors. But good plays don't start with a good actor, they start with a good playwright.

Delivering a presentation well (the acting bit) is a useful skill, and one that can be learnt surprisingly easily, but what really matters is the playwright's skill; the ability to write a great presentation in the first place.

There is a huge extra bonus in concentrating on getting the content right to start with. It isn't just a question of getting the foundation stones in place before you try to put up the building – important though that is. Your involvement in the shaping of the debate from the beginning will shine through at the end. When you make the pitch, the fact that it is your personal vision will radiate. As a consequence, your performance will have much greater confidence. The audience will sense your passion, and that's highly persuasive – if you show real commitment your audience will have trust in your ability to deliver.

Anyone who enjoys the music of the 60s knows that Bob Dylan has pulled off the curious trick of simultaneously having a near-to-dreadful voice yet being a great singer. Listen to any of the covers of his songs by other singers (there are plenty to choose from) and you will find few that match Dylan's emotional power. What makes him a great singer? Answer: the songs he writes are true to his own vision, and that shines through when he sings them.

Don't imagine that writing and owning your presentation means you cannot delegate any of the work to others. Of course you can – good pitches are well researched, well supported by the right data. You can, and should, involve others to share the hard work on this. What you must control is the high ground of the central theme. The great artists of the Renaissance had big studios with plenty of talented helpers who could tick in the details and the backgrounds – but they made sure they had control of the big theme. And they made sure they got the credit.

4 A good pitch starts in your diary

Question: What do business people put in their diaries?
Answer: Business meetings.

PEOPLE MIGHT also put in the odd dentist appointment or a reminder to buy their partner a birthday card, but mostly what they put in is meetings.

And that, when you pause to think about it, is rather odd. Because what they don't put in their diaries is time to plan, time to think. So they are organizing all of their time around only one half of their job, and ignoring the other half.

If you want to succeed at pitching, don't echo that mistake. When you know you need to make a pitch, the first step to eventual success is to create a timetable for yourself. Then book that timetable firmly in your diary.

Make a list of the activities involved in preparing the pitch – there will be information-gathering, meetings with others to discuss ideas, time spent getting slides prepared, time spent on rehearsal. Above all, there needs to be time spent on *thinking*. Work out a timing plan which allows proper time for all these things. This may seem utterly obvious, but in practice it's often neglected. Giving a pitch a proper timetable is motivating to your team, because they quickly have a sense that this important project is being well managed. It will help you too, since pitches generate stress – and having a clear sense of what you have to do, and when by, will take away that stress and replace it with a sense of direction and purpose.

However, creating that timetable is not quite as matter-of-fact and easy as it sounds. If you are going to give proper time to the challenge, you have to stop doing something else. There are still seven days in a week after you took on the pitch project, just like before. To give good time to something new, something old has got to go. It's simple: you have to be ruthless with yourself.

Go through your diary and cancel or postpone everything that isn't utterly crucial.

But you've got to be disciplined about this, or it just won't work. You do want to win this, don't you?

Whatever else goes into your timetable, you must be sure to allocate generous time for *thinking*. Much of the pitch process – collecting data, making slides, rehearsal – is mechanical. You can guess reasonably well how long those tasks will take. But the actual writing of the pitch is not the slightest bit mechanical; it's an imaginative and creative process. That makes it painfully hard to judge how long you need. With creative thinking, it's smart to budget a very generous chunk of time.

There are good reasons for this. First, if you do not allow enough time there is a real risk of an 'Oh my God, I'm not going to get this done...' panic setting in. That will be counter-productive, to say the least. Imaginative creative thinking needs to go down a few blind alleys before it finds the right route. That takes time. Lastly, creative ideas do not arrive when it suits you, creative ideas arrive when it suits them. Like the proverbial London buses, several often arrive in a row – but only after a long wait. So, give time for that wait.

When you have set aside the time, then set aside the space . . .

5 Get your mind and your body to the right space

If you start to write a pitch by sitting down at your usual desk and staring at your usual computer screen, frankly you're doomed.

Unusual thinking doesn't happen when you're in an utterly usual space. You must find a new space to think in

ONE OF the most famous advertising campaigns of recent times, 'Heineken refreshes the parts other beers cannot reach', was written by the talented but eccentric Terry Lovelock, who took himself to the most glamorous hotel in Marrakesh for a fortnight in the hope the muse might visit him. That might seem self-indulgent, but the value to Heineken of an idea that gave personality for a generation to an essentially me-too product makes one hotel bill (albeit a large one, knowing Terry's taste) seem piffling.

In an earlier time, Evelyn Waugh, one of the great English novelists, used to stay in an isolated hotel in Wiltshire to write his works. Less of a hotel than an upmarket B & B, the place was run by a lady with a fondness for literature matched by a steely sense of discipline. She ensured Waugh was not only fed and watered, but also freed from distraction. Thus were *Brideshead Revisited* and *A Handful of Dust* born.

You don't need to escape to Wiltshire, let alone Marrakesh, to find some isolation – but you do need to find it.

For me, simply booking a meeting room in my own offices for a day or two works fine. It's enough to remove me and my thoughts from my usual desk. If it's really important, checking into a hotel near the office and working there can give me a bit more focus.

Some people solve the problem by working on big projects at home. This is cheaper than a hotel and will leave fewer anxieties in your lover's mind, but I find home to be the only place with more distractions than my office desk.

You will find what works for you, but don't make the mistake of thinking this is not critically important to eventual success. It is. There is much at stake in a pitch, and you must have uninterrupted clarity of thought as the foundation stone to build on.

So you need to get yourself into the right space. But you also need to get your mind into the right space. You have to remove the distractions inside your head as well as the distractions around you. I find it impossible to give clear thought to one big challenge if there is an unpaid parking ticket or a trivial but unanswered e-mail adrift in my brain.

My technique to deal with this is simple. I make a list of all my outstanding tasks, be they work or personal. Anything that can safely wait till after the pitch gets set aside, with a note to my secretary to bring it forward to a later date. Anything that can't wait, doesn't. I organize myself to deal with all the can't-wait stuff as ruthlessly as I can before I start thinking about the pitch. It may delay starting on the pitch by a few days, but you would be amazed how much easier and quicker the pitch is when you attack it with a clear mind.

Here's a good example of all this in practice. Early in my advertising career, our young and small agency got the chance to pitch for Volvo's advertising – then, as now, a mighty advertiser. We were given eight weeks to do the job and after six weeks had got precisely nowhere. I was asked to take over the task with just two weeks left.

I got the pitch team in a room and told them that during the first of our two precious weeks, they were forbidden from doing any work on Volvo. What they did have to do was to clear away every other commitment they had, work or social, that was coming over the next two weeks. I wanted to be sure that they could give Volvo attention night and day through the second week.

I then booked a large hotel suite, near the office (but not too near). It was big enough for the team to live, work, sleep and eat in for a week. And that is just what we did.

You would be surprised how much work can be done in a week by a small, bright team giving *total* concentration to one task – with every other distraction taken away.

We won the pitch. My good friend David Abbott was the boss of our small business, and he went on to do famous work for Volvo. He soon started his own company, Abbott Mead Vickers, took Volvo with him, and turned his new company into the largest advertising agency in the UK. So it was worth thinking how to give that pitch the distraction-free space it needed.

6 Shaping your pitch

Have you ever watched a house being built from scratch? For months and months nothing seems to happen – then suddenly the house is there in a matter of weeks. But those months and months of 'nothing' happening are when the site is cleared, the drains put in, the foundations laid. When the base is properly in place, the rest is easy.

IT'S WORTH thinking about that when you draft a pitch. If you get the foundations solidly in place first, and you take a bit of time to do that well, the rest flows naturally. Fail with the foundations and you fail with everything. A good pitch needs a good foundation, a backbone, a central core. That must come first and it must be right.

People often agree with this idea in principle but find it hard to do in practice. They can't resist the temptation to start writing the final pitch before they've really thought through what they want to say.

You must begin at the beginning. A housebuilder starts with a blueprint, not a catalogue of roof-tile designs. You must do the same. I always start with a discussion about the problem and try to pin down what the big issues are –

and if there are more than one or two, you haven't simplified enough.

I have this discussion with a small number of bright colleagues – typically, three or four of us. Beware the committee of six or seven or more: the larger the group the less productive the group dynamic.

I prefer to do this in a room with a whiteboard, so you can draw diagrams of the way the argument unfolds. This makes the debate more involving and helps give it a central focus. I don't know why senior businessmen never have a whiteboard in their offices – they are a huge help in strategic thinking, and if that isn't what senior business people do, what are they there for?

Sometimes you don't want to discuss it with others – either they aren't bright enough or the subject is just too confidential. In that event, I have the discussion with myself. I go on a long walk and talk through in my mind what really matters. Or sometimes I sit in the garden with a large Havana cigar (Hoyo de Monterrey, Epicure No. 1, if you're planning to send me a present) and have a quiet think. Lavish time on this process – the slower and more reflective you are at the start the quicker the process will be at the end. Only when the few big issues are becoming clear should you start to draft the backbone of your argument.

When it comes to drafting, you still need to stay with big issues, to map out the high ground, and to avoid getting sucked into detail. There's a technique which helps hugely in this. I use an artist's A2 layout pad, landscape not portrait, on my table, and I work with a very soft lead artist's pencil, at least 2B. That way you physically can't write in fine detail, so you don't.

You've equipped yourself to write in broad strokes, so you inevitably think in broad strokes.

I then write the outline of the pitch like the storyboard for a film – in a series of frames across the page. In each frame I put only a few words – for example, 'What is the biggest single problem we are trying to solve?'

I usually find, when I start drafting in storyboard form, that I'm clear about the problem and only half-clear about the solution. That doesn't matter: working this way will help to stimulate and crystallize your own thought processes. By the time you get to the solution you'll be clearer on what it is. You will also have spotted gaps in your argument where you need more evidence or more thought to complete your case.

Sketching out your argument in storyboard form seems a bit odd at first. We've been trained since schooldays that the proper form for a train of thought is an essay – or the adult equivalent, a 'paper' or 'report'. But the magic of the storyboard technique is implicit in the name – you shape your argument not just as information but as a story.

Good storytelling is, of course, a visual as well as verbal experience. Because the storyboard was designed to express the storyline of a film, it helps you think visually as well as verbally. That's crucial, especially if you are going to use a medium like PowerPoint. We'll talk more about PowerPoint, the pain and the pleasure, later. The important issue now is that PowerPoint works best when you think of it as a series of pictures.

Each slide is an image which takes the story one thought onward. All too often people write individual slides as if they must exist as a complete message in their own right – they have lots of information but no sense of flow with the slides around them. Think of the slides as stepping stones in an argument. They don't need meaning in themselves; they have meaning when they follow in a sequence. In fact they are often much more interesting when they don't have meaning on their own, because then you want to know what happens next. Which takes us back to where we began – great pitches are designed not as information but as storytelling.

7 Understanding structure – and why Chopin has more in common with the Coldstream Guards than you might expect

You might – not unreasonably – imagine that the Coldstream Guards and Chopin had little in common, other than the initial letter 'C'. Clearly, one of the world's great composers and one of Britain's crack regiments might have excellence in common, but it's hard to see what else.

THERE IS one other thing they share, however, and it's surprisingly important. Chopin had a clear grasp of structure in the music he composed. Similarly, when one of the British army's top regiments goes into battle it knows that success depends greatly on clear communication of plans and orders; and that in turn depends on an understanding of structure in communications.

Chopin is greatly admired for his sonatas. The sonata form

follows a very definite structure. A sonata begins with *exposition* (the composer setting out his idea), follows with *development* (the idea is developed and explored) and ends with *recapitulation* (the idea is re-expressed).

The British army has been one of the more successful organizations in the last five hundred years of history. How they communicate is worth studying.

The army doctrine on this is brilliantly simple:

Say what you're going to say.
Say it.
Say it again.

Look carefully at the army's refreshingly simple approach to communication and then look at the structure of a sonata. They're strangely similar, aren't they?

Both start with a setting out of the idea; both then deliver that idea; both then summarize that idea.

When you ask someone to *structure* a presentation, they often seem unclear as to what that really means. What it means is that you must give shape to your argument. An argument is like any other construction – it needs some basic architecture to hold it clearly in place.

Watching people working on pitches, I'm often struck by how easily they get obsessed with detail. Which, inevitably, means that they are not looking at the big picture – particularly whether there is a clear shape to their argument.

Stand back from your pitch and make sure it has structure.
To get that structure right, you can defer to Chopin and use
the sonata form – *exposition, development, recapitulation* –
or you can defer to the British army and their rubric for
good communication – *say what you're going to say, say it,
say it again*. Either way, you get the same answer. And, like
all good answers, it's not only right, it's also both simple
and universal.

As a postscript, we started with a question on whether
Chopin and the Coldstream Guards had anything in
common beyond an initial 'C'. We could add one more 'C'
to that list: *cinéma-vérité*, the great French film-making
movement. Jean-Luc Godard, a pillar of *cinéma-vérité* and
one of cinema's great directors, said firmly that a film
should have 'a beginning, a middle, and an end'.
Provocatively, he added, 'Though not necessarily in that
order.'

Godard delighted in subverting conventional structure, but
he knew that even he had to have a structure to subvert.

8 Tell your story, from problem to solution

People readily accept the idea that a presentation needs structure. Yet they often still don't quite grasp what that should look like in practice. We've agreed a pitch is telling a story – but what is the theme of that story?

A PITCH STORY must be one of problem and solution. Most pitches contain an unending load of information, but precious little persuasion. Why? Because they are constructed in a business mindset of facts, data, information. You must free yourself from that. Don't concentrate on the data, concentrate on the *problem*.

Your audience have a problem they want to solve. They are not in the room with you as a favour to you, they are there because they're worried about a problem, and you might – just might – be able to solve it for them. So when you construct your pitch, construct it as a story – not just any story, but a story of problem and resolution.

Don't be shy about dwelling on their problem. Define it, discuss it, deliberate over it.

When you are ill, there is nothing more reassuring than a doctor who can talk to you about your symptoms as accurately as you can. It creates a wonderful sense of empathy and trust.

The same applies in business. A good pitch starts with a crystal-clear exposition of the problem you are trying to solve. The unspoken response you want in the minds of your audience is: 'He may not have solved it yet, but this guy really knows what our problem is.' That quickly leads to the feeling: 'If he understands the problem well, I trust him on the answer.'

Then elaborate. Develop your understanding of that problem. Show some research, some statistics, even some anecdotal insights, which dramatize that problem. The purpose of this stage is plain: it is to make your audience gut-wrenchingly, suicidally miserable about the scale of their problem.

Why? Because a doctor who cures a headache will be remembered for a moment, but a doctor who cures a cancer will be remembered for a lifetime.

The bigger the problem, the more valuable the solution.

Once you have really brought your audience down, you need to start showing them the answer. But don't be timid about labouring the point on bringing them down first. You are talking to people for whom the 3.6 per cent sales decline in the south-west sales region is as important – perhaps more important – than global warming or the nuclear threat from North Korea. People take their jobs hugely seriously: they wouldn't be able to do them otherwise. So worry with them for a while. After all, if you take their worries seriously you are taking them seriously.

Having proved yourself their equal in anxiety, you now need to prove yourself their superior in solution. Sympathetic diagnosis is all very well, but then you have to offer treatment.

This needs to be gradual. A striptease is not sexy if it's done in a hurry. However, before we debate too much about how to reveal your solution, you need to have a solution in the first place.

Finding the right solution to a business problem is usually hampered by the expectation that the answer has to have some unique 'Eureka!' factor.

Don't worry about that for a nano-second. The solution to most business problems is usually not some astonishing breakthrough idea. It is more often a healthy dose of pragmatic common sense, underscored by some real passion about delivery. We'll talk more, later, about how the *least worst solution* is by definition the *best solution*.

The big point for now is to understand that it is not the originality of the idea which drives most business successes, it is the commitment to making the idea happen.

9 Make simplicity an obsession

Set yourself this test. Imagine that you are the audience for a pitch, and you have to choose between two presentations.

THE FIRST presentation has a good solution to your problem, but you lack trust and confidence in the presenter. The second presentation has not yet got a convincing solution but, in spite of that, the presenter is inspiring.

Whom do you choose? Experience tells me that most audiences will choose the second presenter: they would rather back the individual than the solution. They will rationalize, quite correctly, that the right solution may never get airborne if it is driven by the wrong person. But the right person will find the right solution even if that hasn't yet happened. And they want to work with someone they believe in.

In short, the key to understanding pitching is to understand that it is the pitcher who is on trial, not the presentation.

We have already talked about the crucial importance of inspiring confidence. But how do you do that?

It's easier than you might think. Your audience wants to

back a winner. So you have to look like a winner. How do winners behave, that sets them apart from ordinary mortals?

Winners, like any other category of human being, come in all shapes and sizes. Yet they do tend to have four things in common:

- They set their sights high; they are ambitious.
- They are pragmatic. Ambitious they may be, but they are not dreamers.
- They concentrate on the big issues. They get others to do the detail.
- They keep it simple.

You can learn from all of these strengths, but the last is hugely important.

Winners instinctively know that to make something big happen, you've got to concentrate on the few things that really matter. That is why they keep it simple.

We can observe that respect for simplicity, but it is often hard to emulate. In preparing a pitch it's all too easy to want to show that you're thorough, that you've covered every contingency. I've even seen people boast about the sheer size of a pitch document, as if 'How big is the book?' means the same as 'How big is the idea within it?'

The truth is that being thorough may get you on the shortlist, but it will never win it for you. One strong, central idea beats a thousand pages of analysis every time. So focus on what matters and ruthlessly throw out anything that gets in the way.

Do you have slides with masses of information? Ditch them. Does your argument wander at all? Rethink it. Do you need more than a sentence to sum up your big idea? Start again – it's almost certainly not a big idea yet.

The simpler your idea and the simpler your presentation of it, then the more likely you are to emerge the winner.

10 Have you got the perfect answer?

When you draft a pitch, you often find that the problem seems to come across more convincingly than the solution. You shouldn't worry about that too much.

IN HOLLYWOOD, and in our dreams, solutions are dazzlingly right and instantly effective. In real life, however, there's rarely a silver bullet which solves everything. It's surprisingly often the case that, given a choice of imperfect answers, the 'least worst' route isn't just the best of the bunch – it also works in practice.

And working in practice is what matters. Theory is fine, and it makes a living for management consultants, but when faced with a problem you'll achieve far more by getting on and doing something than by searching endlessly for perfection.

There is no truer dictum than 'a bad decision on Monday makes more money than a good decision on Friday'.

That's why you shouldn't be frightened of the 'least worst'

route. It's true in life as well as business: an answer that's not utterly perfect but is *pragmatic* and therefore leads to *action* is an answer that will deliver for you.

When you're searching for the perfect solution in your pitch, don't forget that your audience want to be more than just an audience: they want to take part, to bring something to the debate.

Paradoxically, an imperfect answer gives your audience much more opportunity to contribute to the discussion than an apparently faultless solution – even if such a thing exists.

We said earlier that a good pitch is a kind of storytelling. Part of the magic of reading a good book is that the reader brings his imagination into play, and so adds to the story. If your pitch works well, the same thing will happen. Your audience will get involved and start to add their own light and shade. That's when you know you've won.

11 The cornerstone slide

When the British Government first put the running of the National Lottery out to pitch, they offered a massive prize. The company which won would have an instant monopoly of a colossal business. Not surprising then that so many blue-chip companies joined the race. One of these was Camelot, a consortium of major British businesses and the largest US lottery-running organization.

WHILE OTHER bidders thought hard about what they wanted to say in their bid, Camelot thought hard about what the British Government (judge and jury in this case) would want to hear. They reasoned that government officials are not like entrepreneurial businessmen, who are driven by the hope of success. On the contrary, civil servants are driven by the fear of failure. Camelot realized that they needed to persuade their audience less by the promise that things would go right and more by the reassurance that things would not go wrong.

That simple, but potent, insight became the core of Camelot's campaign. The central theme of their pitch was 'We won't let you down'. Not an inspiring call to arms, you

may think, but then you aren't a government official.
Everything that Camelot did and said in their pitch was
designed to reinforce this message of reassurance and
dependability.

Camelot won the bid, comfortably and confidently. They
went on to make a controversially large amount of money
out of the contract. And it's a contract they still hold, nearly
a quarter of a century later.

We can learn from Camelot's experience. Certainly they
were shrewd in understanding the mood of their audience.
But, important though that was, their shrewdness went
beyond that. They realized the value of having – even in a
pitch as large and complex as the lottery bid – one strong
but simple idea at the heart of everything.

When you write a pitch, be sure that you have a powerful
idea at its core. Then be sure that the central idea is
crystal clear to your audience – because if it's not vivid to
them, it might as well not be there.

Go through your draft presentation and *identify the one
slide that encapsulates this central idea*. If it's a good pitch,
that slide will be there. I call it the 'cornerstone slide'.
Make sure it's as clear, as crisp and as simple as it can be.
Then, when you deliver the presentation, linger on that
slide and say,

'If you forget everything else but
remember this slide, you'll still
have captured the essence of
what we're saying to you.'

The effect is dramatic. You will, in a moment, convince your audience that your pitch has a big idea at its heart. Nothing can be more compelling.

Of course, you may go through your draft pitch and fail to find your cornerstone slide. That could be the symptom of a lesser illness: your pitch has a central idea, but it is not expressed well. Or it could even be the symptom of a much more serious disease: your pitch does not have that vital central idea. Whichever is the case, it is better to know while you can still do something about it. Because if your pitch does not radiate a strong theme, however worthy it may be in other ways, it is simply not going to win for you. You will have to tear it up and start again. That's painful but not as painful as failure.

So the message is simple. Be sure your pitch has a strong central idea. Be sure it is encapsulated well in one slide. Then use that cornerstone slide in your delivery to dramatize the simplicity and strength of your promise.

12 The two-edged sword called the 'executive summary'

Should a pitch have a summary?

A ND A subsidiary question: What is the difference between a plain unvarnished 'summary' and an 'executive summary'?

The answer to the second question is easy enough. There's absolutely no difference between an 'executive summary' and a 'summary'. Except perhaps that one is a term used by people who like two words where one would do, and are so unconfident that they see business jargon as a kind of linguistic security blanket. I did once witness a debate between two grown men, incredibly, as to whether it was better to say 'management summary' or 'executive summary'. Clearly, there's no difference as they are both equally pretentious.

Having established that we should call a summary what it is, a summary, does a pitch need one?

The answer is a little more complex than you might expect. It has to do with the order of play in a pitch, and how that relates to the transfer of power a pitch is designed to achieve.

A summary at the end of a pitch can be invaluable. A good

pitch has a strong central idea, but it may also have to cover a wide range of related issues. You may need to demonstrate comprehensiveness as well as clarity. You may have to show a grasp of detail as well as strategic flair. In short, your pitch may have to cover a wide sweep of ground, which scores highly for thoroughness but makes it harder to keep a sharp focus on the main message. A summary can help you pull back from the comprehensiveness and the detail to the few big issues. It can also help you reinforce the underlying logic in your argument by reiterating it in simplified form.

Above all, it gives you the chance to restate your central theme in crisp, simple terms.

To do that well, remember that you are summarizing the argument, not the supporting facts.

So, have a summary, and work hard on it – it may well get more scrutiny than any other part of the pitch.

However, that summary must – repeat, must – come at the end of the pitch.

There is a fashion amongst some who should know better (investment bankers are, unsurprisingly, the worst culprits) for having the summary at the start of the pitch. Start with the summary, they say, and we can all see quickly what the main issues are. Indeed they can – which is precisely why they must not be allowed to.

A good pitch unfolds like a good story. And a good pitcher controls his audience as that story unfolds. If the summary comes first, none of that can happen.

The audience won't get involved in a story if they know at the outset what happens at the end. So the pitcher loses control. That is why some audiences like to start with the summary – they wrest control from the pitcher. That is also why the pitcher must not give in to this pressure.

In summary (dare I say?): have a summary; keep it clear; keep it simple. Above all, put it at the end of the pitch, where it keeps the power with you, the pitcher.

13 Confidence is the key

A pitch always calls for decisions to be made about the future: Will you employ me? Will you marry me? Will you fund my new project?

WHEN THE audience to a pitch try to deal with questions like these, they have to look into the future and imagine how things will be months and years after their decision has been taken. But obviously they can never know how the future will unfold – all they can do is make a best guess as the basis for their answer. Therefore their confidence in the person asking the question is crucial in how they form their answer.

If a bank is asked to fund a new venture, the bankers can never know how the venture will work in practice: but they do know whether they trust the person asking for the funds. Again and again, when people are asked to back a plan, in reality they are being asked to back the person behind the plan. That's why trust and confidence are so important. If the person asking the question is the kind of person who inspires confidence, he is likely to get the answer he wants. And vice versa. So the ability to radiate confidence is crucial.

To test this point, ask yourself what is the toughest pitch question ever asked. It must be, 'Will you marry me?' No other pitch question has two lifetimes of human happiness at stake. Yet this is the pitch question which usually gets the fastest and most certain answer. Why? Because when we answer a pitch question we're really rating our belief in whoever is asking the question – and your belief in someone is never greater than when you're in love with them.

The issue of confidence can be taken as a given in romance, but it certainly can't anywhere else; especially if money is involved. And many important pitches are related directly to money: Will you buy my business? Will you invest in this new idea? Many other pitches are related indirectly to money – a job interview is essentially a test of whether the employer is willing to risk the cost of a salary on a particular candidate.

When money is involved, there lies a problem. If you are asking for money, you must be talking to someone who has money; and the bigger the amount you are asking for, the more your audience must have.

And people who have money tend to have one characteristic in common: they want to keep it. The more money they have, the more passionately they want to keep it.

When you think about it, it's not surprising – the people who are most willing to take risks are the ones with nothing to lose. So the bigger your pitch is, in terms of the money involved, the more likely it is that your audience will be cautious and risk-averse. Therefore, for them, the whole issue of confidence in you becomes absolutely overwhelming.

If they don't have confidence in you, they certainly won't have confidence in your idea.

Confidence is also a very infectious condition. As is the lack of confidence. The old joke is that a football manager is usually fired within a week of the club chairman making a public declaration of confidence in him. This is cruelly true, but there is a reason for it. The only time a chairman would need to make a statement of confidence in his manager is when that confidence is in doubt. If everything was fine, he wouldn't need to say a thing. The very fact that the chairman makes the declaration of confidence in his manager is actually an admission that it's an issue; that his confidence is in question. Since lack of confidence grows like a weed, it's no surprise that a week after the chairman's statement, the manager is on his way.

When a politician is forced to resign, the process is often similar. It's not so much that he's guilty of one big crime: it's more a question of accumulating lack of public confidence in him. That makes his position ultimately untenable; and the Prime Minister who was offering statements of confidence in the man in late February is announcing his resignation in early March.

This all begs the big question – how can you radiate confidence? First, by not trying too hard. People who look as if they are desperate to reassure you only end up looking desperate. That certainly inspires no confidence. Part of the challenge is to look as if it doesn't matter that much. Yes, of course you want to win the pitch, otherwise you wouldn't be there – but it's not life and death.

Second, confidence is about generating from previous behaviour a suggestion that future behaviour will be dependable. At the heart of every pitch is a question about the future. People are much more comfortable answering that question if they have some relevant examples from the past. So the clever pitcher finds ways of demonstrating that their previous work and their previous experience should encourage their audience to trust them for the future. What you have done yesterday proves what you can do tomorrow.

Confidence is also about dealing with your audience as if you are an equal, not a supplicant. Of course you need to treat your audience with courtesy. But if you deal with them in a way that suggests the balance of power lies with them, you are saying that the balance of power does not lie with you. In other words, they have strength, you have weakness. And if you are weak, why on earth should you inspire confidence? So your tone and your body language must suggest that we are all looking at this problem as equals together.

Another key to confidence is not to need the deal too much. If you radiate a sense that you want to win, then that's fine. But if you radiate a sense that you need to win, then that's a weakness. The audience must always feel that you can live without them. There's nothing more sexy than a hint of hard-to-get, and there is nothing less sexy than being too eager to please. As every woman knows, if you are too available you lose your magic.

Confidence is also tied up with simplicity. If you express yourself simply, it inspires confidence.

Complicated arguments, millions of statistics, pages of analysis – these are not the trappings of a confident leader; they are the trappings of an insecure middle-management drudge. The more complex the reassurances you give, the less reassuring you become. Inspiring confidence is about taking the higher ground.

There is a paradox here. Inspiring confidence is also about reassuring people that things won't go wrong. To do that, your audience want to know that there is depth and detail behind your capture of the high ground. So even though the good pitcher concentrates on articulating the big issue simply, he must still demonstrate that the detail has been taken care of. The trick is for the leader to show that while he has command of the strategy and the big idea, he has strong support troops who can give him all the technical and tactical back-up he needs.

It's a sad joke of the advertising business – an arena where pitches are an especially important part of life – that the advertisements shown in the winning pitch are very rarely the advertisements which end up being used in real life.

This is not, I believe, because the client always changes his mind about what makes a good ad. It's because the client wasn't looking for a good ad in the first place. He was looking for good people and the ads were a way of testing the quality of those people. The issue at stake is not his confidence in the advertising, it's his confidence in the people who'll be producing it.

To prove this, talk to advertising agency clients about how they respond to pitches. One of their most frequently voiced anxieties is that the people who impress them in the presentation won't be the people they work with afterwards. Nothing could demonstrate more vividly that they are not really buying an answer, they are buying people they can trust.

Postscript: when adman Tim Bell, a heavy smoker, went to work for Margaret Thatcher's first election campaign she politely explained that 10 Downing Street was a no-smoking zone. Tim replied, with his infectious chuckle, that in that case he would have to put someone else on the project. Mrs Thatcher gave in. Tim's unwillingness to compromise, even over an apparently footling issue, suggested a strength which radiated confidence.

14 The tyranny of PowerPoint

The foundation stone of a great pitch is writing it well – but it still has to be articulated to its audience. The message needs a medium. The vast majority of presentations today are done on PowerPoint. Yet PowerPoint is to communications what a microwave is to cooking – living proof that 'easier' is not always the same as 'better'. And just as a microwave is the perfect short cut to bland food, so PowerPoint is the perfect short cut to bland thought.

I
T NEEDN'T be: PowerPoint is actually an astoundingly valuable tool – provided you are the master and PowerPoint is the servant. But to make it work for you, rather than you work for it, it's important to understand its strengths and its shortcomings.

The strengths are easy to understand. You can produce a presentation very fast, and it looks professional. The trouble is that looking and being professional are not at all the same thing. And that's PowerPoint's big weakness – because it's easy to use quickly, it discourages thought.

You concentrate on making the slide look right, not on what it is saying.

A modern digital camera, with automatic focus, automatic exposure, automatic wind-on, automatic anything-else-you-can-think-of, enables you to take dozens of snaps, very quickly, all with good focus and the right exposure. Trouble is, none of the shots are ever really great photographs – because it's too easy and you haven't thought about them. Professional photographers often use digital cameras nowadays – but the cameras they use allow them to control focus, exposure, and so on. The professional photographer thinks about and plans his shot before he takes it.

You need to use PowerPoint the same way. Be a professional photographer, not an amateur: recognize that planning must come before doing. Get the content of the presentation absolutely right first – and there is no substitute for writing it out longhand – and then treat the PowerPoint programme as you treat the Word programme. It's simply a device for setting out your thoughts.

A noted American academic, Edward R. Tufte, has written a whole book devoted to a savage attack on the evils of PowerPoint. While you have to admire his dedication, I take issue with him. I agree that PowerPoint can be dreadful, but my reasons are different from Tufte's. He thinks that PowerPoint is evil because it simplifies too much. I think it's evil because it doesn't simplify enough. Because it's easy to add bits – such as extra colours or a logo in the corner – bits get added. But all they do is make the presentation more cluttered, because there's too much stuff in it. This happens when you compose the slide on your laptop straight into the PowerPoint programme. No wonder *how it looks* and *what it says* get muddled.

Whenever I see people in my own office struggling on their PCs over a pitch, I always notice the same thing – they're trying to write the pitch straight into PowerPoint slides. It's a bit like trying to paint a picture and get it framed at the same time.

The only way is to write the presentation away from your computer. When it's finished, then transpose it into PowerPoint. Better yet, ask someone else to put it into PowerPoint for you. Then, when you check it, you won't be thinking: 'What pretty slides I've made', you'll be thinking: 'Do these slides say what I want them to say?'

I mentioned the logo-in-the-corner thing earlier. What is that about? Again and again I see pitches, from advertising agencies for example, where every single slide has the agency logo in one corner and the client logo in another. Are they so insecure they think the client will forget where he is? I have the street number of my house on the front door, but I don't have it on every door inside as well. And if I write you a letter, the top page will have my letterhead on it, but it won't be tediously repeated on every page which follows. No, the logo-in-the-corner obsession is partly because PowerPoint makes it easy to do; so you do it. It's also due to a lack of confidence about keeping every slide as simple as possible.

First cousin to the logo-in-the-corner obsession is the can-we-have-a-coloured-background fetish. Again, it's due to a fear of simplicity. Great communication is simple communication – but it takes courage and confidence to keep it simple.

When you go to a good restaurant, the dish you ordered looks good but simple when it's served. Go to a bad restaurant, and the dish you ordered will arrive drowning in garnish and salad. They don't have the confidence to keep it simple.

That confidence is a power you must have; but it doesn't come from some kind of blind bravery. It comes from knowing that what you are saying is strong in its own right, so it doesn't need to be dressed up. Indeed, dressing it up will detract from your message, not add to it.

To achieve that clear belief in what you are saying, it is crucial to get the structure and content of your argument right before you start worrying about how you show that argument.

Only when you truly know what you want to say, and not before, should you start to think how you say it. That way, you'll be using PowerPoint instead of PowerPoint using you.

Of course, there are other ways of doing it – you don't have to use PowerPoint. In business, pitches are almost always done on PowerPoint. Why? Because it's the convention, and for no other reason. In politics, pitches are almost always done as speeches with no visual aids. Why? Because it's the convention, and for no other reason. In both politics and business, pitches are done today the way they were done yesterday. We just aren't thinking hard enough about choosing a medium which works for our particular message. All that said, while I hate PowerPoint when it's used badly (which is most of the time) I like it greatly when it's used well. If you don't want to use PowerPoint, first decide why that is. If it's because you're frightened of PowerPoint, take it on and win. If you have a deeper reason, look at the alternatives.

A great alternative – if you're confident enough – is simply to use a big pad or a whiteboard and write up the key messages of your presentation as you go along. This does not, repeat not, work if the presentation is not short and simple. It also does not, absolutely not, work if the presenter is not on top of his material. But for a good presenter with a simple pitch, its sense of spontaneity is irresistible. What's so good about writing your charts as you go is that it demonstrates not only a real grasp of your material, but huge confidence. And *confidence* is infectious.

Another interesting alternative is to have only about two or three charts, prepared smartly on board, and use them to illustrate the crucial points of your talk. Again, this technique needs a simple pitch and a confident presenter.

The one technique to avoid at any price is to present by giving everyone in the group a bound book of the presentation slides, and taking them through it page by page. A key to good pitching is to control your audience. How you pace the presentation, how you deal with questions, above all *how you let the argument unfold* must be in your hands and no one else's. This can't happen if everyone is going through the book – an accountant will have turned to the numbers in the back, been horrified by the size of the proposed investment, and turned against you, long before you've even been able to describe the benefits of the investment.

Pitch whatever way you like as long as it isn't 'going

through the book'. That said, it's a frequently used method, because it seems easy and people are lazy. But you must be strong enough to resist it. Even when the laptop has a glitch and you can't show your slides, better to make them wait for half an hour while IT fix it than get trapped into using the book. When you lose control you lose everything.

The truth is that PowerPoint is very often the best medium to use.

> But to make it work for you, remember that you must write the presentation first. Only when your draft is perfect do you start translating it into PowerPoint.

And when you do, remember that great truism 'less is more'. And while you're at it, remember that if a saying has graduated to being a truism, it's probably for that simple reason: it's true.

15 The art of rehearsal – and why you don't leave it till the night before

The legendary golfer Gary Player was once accused of being lucky.

'Yes,' he agreed, 'and the harder I practise the luckier I get.'

Great performers know that talent is most of it, but it's not all of it. Raw talent gives you the opportunity, but it is hard work and practice that enable you to seize that opportunity.

THAT IS as true of winning at presentations as it is of winning at golf. (And there's just as much pride and money at stake in business at the highest level as in golf at the highest level.) Practice matters – but how do you go about it?

In the art of presentation, practice means rehearsal. And rehearsal is curiously hard to do. If we rehearse on our own, there is a constant anxiety that someone will barge into the meeting room, catch you talking to yourself, and walk out again muttering clichés about the first sign of madness. If you rehearse in front of your colleagues – well, if you've done it, you'll know what I mean – it's quite the most embarrassing experience you could imagine. And knowing that, you don't do it well, which makes the embarrassment worse, and so the vicious spiral feeds on itself.

The unvarnished truth is that rehearsing pitches makes us feel uncomfortable, and because it makes us feel uncomfortable we do as little of it as we dare. If *Homo sapiens* was a species with more courage, we would identify the demons that frighten us, confront them and destroy them. But it often seems easier to hide.

Except that there isn't anywhere to hide. We are going to have to give this presentation to its eventual audience anyway. And if we are worried about feeling uncomfortable, there are few things more uncomfortable-making than delivering a bad pitch to an influential audience. So we must rise above the average level of *Homo sapiens* and learn to do something most of our colleagues are notoriously weak at. We must learn to grasp the nettle.

Like it or not, we are going to rehearse. And we are going to do it thoroughly and well. Like most things in life that we don't like doing, it quickly becomes easier once we start to do it. But it also helps to understand the technique of how rehearsal can help us.

Rehearsal is not just about practice, it's about practice with a purpose. Practice with two purposes, in fact, since rehearsal on your own achieves something quite different from rehearsal with others.

Let's start with rehearsal with others – and that usually

means others in your team, others working on the same pitch. We have already defined this as one of life's truly awkward moments. There is a simple way to deal with that – don't even try to 'deliver' the pitch, just go through it. Be clear at the outset that your aim is not to rehearse your delivery, but to get their views on the content.

Your team may be an impossibly embarrassing audience on whom to test delivery, but they can be hugely helpful as constructive critics of content. They will know enough about the subject to spot flaws in the argument, but they will not – unlike you – be so close to the issue that they can no longer judge it objectively.

Go through it with them slowly (in non-delivery mode), encouraging them to identify weaknesses in the argument, and be a good listener. That doesn't just mean listening to what they say, it also means disciplining yourself not to react defensively when they say it. Note their criticisms, literally writing the points down. Written notes give you a record for later; but they also force you to think before you react.

When it's all over, reflect on their comments and separate ones you agree with from the rest. Asking their opinion doesn't oblige you to share it, but some of what they say will be worth thinking about. If you can't decide on a particular issue, back your own judgement, not theirs. A huge part of winning at pitches is about confidence, and you might as well start working on that now.

Rehearsing with colleagues is not a test of delivery – it never can be, it simply won't work – but it is a crucial test of content. You need to understand that, and they need to understand that too. Once you all have that shared view of what you are trying to achieve, you will achieve it well.

If you can't test your delivery of a pitch with this kind of rehearsal, how can you?

This is where rehearsing on your own becomes important. On your own, there is no one to laugh at you, no one looking at their watch for the next meeting. You can deal with your pitch however you want, and if you want to go through the same bit twenty-six times before you're happy with it, you can.

This is why rehearsing on your own is key to achieving good delivery. You should choose a place and a time where you won't be disturbed. I find it easiest at home, or late in the office when the others have gone, but whatever works for you is the right answer.

Then, imagine this is the moment and deliver your pitch. If you stumble on a bit (and you will), go back and start again.

Go on, again and again, until it feels right to you.

One of your aims in this is to memorize the order of your argument. That does not mean that you learn your script parrot-fashion. You should not have a rigid word-by-word script in the first place. (A rigid script sounds just that – rigid.) What you should have is a clear sense of the flow of the argument, and which point follows which. A good technique is to write down in two or three words the theme of each slide, and use that as your 'script'. Get this order of argument imprinted in your mind by endless rehearsal, and you will always seem confident and on top of your material when the big day comes.

Time your pitch, and check if it seems to be taking too long. But, if it does, don't speed up your delivery – a fast talker seems more anxious to get to the end than to make the point. And a fast talker inhibits the audience from asking questions. A good pitch feels like a dialogue, not a lecture, so your ability to encourage questions and deal with them on the journey is important.

So an unhurried pace of delivery is vital. But it's also vital that it doesn't all go on too long. What happens when you can't reconcile one with the other?

The answer is painfully simple. If your presentation takes too long, it is too long. Shorten it. Weed out the bits which are 'nice to have' but not central to the argument.

'I can't do that,' I hear you cry. But you can, and you must. Virtually every presentation suffers from having too much of what the speaker wants to say, rather than what the audience need to hear.

The stuff which takes up so much time (the self-justifying facts and figures, evidence of work done rather than evidence of solutions uncovered) can easily be put in an appendix for discussion later, if needed.

So be ruthless. If your private rehearsal suggests that you're taking too long to make the point, it's probably because you are. Distil and simplify.

The shorter and simpler your case, the more confidence you radiate.

Pitches which exude confidence often win; pitches which

fail to never do. That confidence can only come from endless rehearsal.

Rehearsal with colleagues will get you confident about the content. You need to do that a good few days before the pitch, to give time to rework content.

Rehearsal on your own, seemingly without end, will get you confident about delivery. You need to do that about a day before. It needs to be fresh in your mind on the day that matters. Besides, nobody ever got an important pitch ready for dress rehearsal more than a day in advance.

Shouldn't you rehearse the night before? No, just get an early night and wake up fresh. Late-night workaholism may assuage your guilt, but it won't improve your performance.

The night before Waterloo, Napoleon took his officers through the battle plans one more time, as they had a lot to fight for. Wellington told his officers to get an early night, as they had a long day ahead of them.

Wellington won.

16 The pitch itself

A great deal of winning at pitching is about getting it right beforehand – understanding the audience, thinking through a clear position, writing a pitch which has clarity and a big idea.

THAT'S TRUE, but you still have to perform well on the day. Even that is in large part due to preparation in advance. As the chapter on rehearsal makes clear, if you are master of your subject on the day then you inspire confidence – and the only way to be master of your subject on the day is to rehearse tirelessly beforehand.

But the day still matters. There are only a few things you need to concentrate on:

- How you pace and shape the presentation
- How you deal with questions
- The use of humour

In all of these, your body language will say as much as the words you use.

Body language is a term often used with a mixture of uncertainty and awe as if it was some obscure skill which could only be taught by Buddhists in California. Actually, it's a straightforward mixture of courtesy and common sense. If you present with your hand in your pocket, it just looks a bit scruffy. If you present sitting down, rather than standing up, it makes it much harder to dominate and control your audience.

All you really have to do is to remember two things: you are in charge of your audience; and you are there for them. A few years ago a Conservative Party Constituency Association were interviewing candidates for a safe seat. Whoever won the interview won a seat in the House of Commons. The room was set with a row of chairs for the eight interviewers, facing a lectern for the interviewee. The first seven interviewees entered in turn, each placed their notes on the lectern, each stood behind the lectern, each gave their prepared speech.

The eighth came in, ignored the lectern by standing in front of it, and gave a fluent speech without any notes. He dealt more naturally, more confidently, more instinctively with his audience. He won their nomination and went on to win the seat. His name was David Cameron and he went on not just to win the seat, but to become prime minister.

If you look at people when you're talking to them and – even more importantly – look at people closely when they ask you something, then you can't help conveying a sense that you are interested, that they are important to you. This is body language working for you.

Note-taking is another area where you can use body language to help you. To my mind there is nothing more irritating than presenting to someone who is constantly taking notes throughout your presentation. It gives the impression that he is recording what you are saying, but not listening to it. But if you take no notes *until an important point is made and then make a note of that*, your body language shows real involvement with the issue. And it flatters the speaker wonderfully.

This brings us to the question of speakers using notes. It's very simple: *Don't*. Few things in life are more unconvincing than a speaker who is constantly referring to his notes. It's a living advertisement for the fact that that he doesn't have a full grasp of the issues. So don't have any notes; then you can't refer to them. That does make it harder to deliver the presentation, assuming you can't be bothered to rehearse it properly. But if you want to win, you will be bothered to rehearse it thoroughly. And if you do rehearse it thoroughly, you won't need notes.

Does that mean you learn the whole speech off by heart and deliver it as an actor delivers his lines, speaking every single word as written by the author? The answer is no, of course not. If you don't stray from your own script and extemporize around it, you will come across as rigid and unconfident. But if you rehearse your material thoroughly enough, you will feel sufficiently confident to interrupt your own flow occasionally.

In the chapter on rehearsal, I said that I find it useful to make a list of the key issues in the presentation – the chapter headings, if you like – in the order in which they occur. I do this as part of my rehearsal process to help me memorize the sequence of my story. The point is that I am not learning a script (which stifles spontaneity), I am learning the train of thought. I refer to it endlessly up to the minute I stand on stage. But then the notes go in my pocket, and I always do the pitch without notes. That way, I can pause, digress for a moment, take a question, and still return to the main theme at the right point because the structure of the pitch is clearly embedded in my mind.

What about autocue? The answer is no, no, no, a thousand times no.

Autocue combines the stilted lack of spontaneity that comes from referring to notes with the ghastly and wooden rigidity that comes from reading a script word for word. It is, after all, no more than an electronic script and note machine.

Companies who arrange presentations often insist on autocues, but don't be misled into thinking they are there to help you. They are there only to help the presentation company, because they are responsible for clicking up the next PowerPoint slide at the right moment, and autocue tells them when to do that. For this to work, you have to stick resolutely to the prepared script, otherwise the slide operator will lose his place. Hello, lifeless clinical efficiency; goodbye, human warmth and passion.

The technique for dealing with this is very simple. First, you flatly refuse to have an autocue. Second, you insist that you have control of the button which moves on the slide. Then you know you are doing it at the right place, and at the right pace.

The audience will see the difference immediately: you'll look like a public speaker in charge of his material, not an automaton – and they'll love you for it.

The pace and handling of a pitch are crucial. You must give people the sense that the meeting is for them, not for you. So if they want to spend a long time talking about something you think is minor, go with it.

Obviously you need to control your agenda, but you need to do so in a way which makes them feel this is a dialogue not a lecture.

It may become clear in the meeting that a part of your pitch is not as interesting to them as you expected. Recognize that; say so; and don't linger on it. The fact that a slide is in the presentation doesn't mean it has to be discussed – especially if they don't want to. A degree of spontaneity is vital if people are going to feel good about you and good about working with you.

The next issue in pacing a presentation relates to the number of slides and the length of time you speak for. It's often assumed that presentations with lots of slides are longer. That is often not true. I have seen people spend ten minutes on one slide; and I've seen people go through half a dozen slides in less than a minute. It's much more important that each slide is simple and is a stepping-stone to the next slide. Then the presentation will flow quickly.

Using plenty of slides is not a problem if you move through them crisply. What is a problem is lingering endlessly on one slide. You've got to keep a sense of movement – but not a sense of rush. That depends partly on how you present, but it also depends on how the presentation was written in the first place.

Don't be afraid to click through a few slides almost without mentioning them if you think that suits the mood of the meeting. It suggests that you know what's less important – and therefore that you know what's more important.

People often judge a presentation by how long it lasts. That really isn't the issue; as the old joke has it:

> 'Was it a long presentation?'
> 'No, it just felt like that.'

It is not about how long you are there, it is about how you feel when you are there. If you want to make it feel long and tedious, there is no better way than to read out every word on a slide.

The human eye can read a slide much faster than the human voice can speak it. So don't speak it. They know what's on it already. What you need to do is to focus on the key point the slide is making. Try to do this with words which are slightly different from the ones on the screen. You are a commentator, an interpreter even, not a reader.

Every piece of advice I have ever seen about presenting makes this same warning – never, ever read out the slides. Yet people still do, and it's still beyond dull when they do.

Body language really matters when you have to deal with questions. A pitch is a good pitch when people start taking an active part in the process. So questions matter greatly. They are not an intrusion, they are involvement. Deal with them straightaway. Saying 'I'd rather answer that at the end' sounds overly formal; and it implies that your timetable is more important than his question. If he asks the question now, now might be the time he'd like the answer.

There is one exception to this. Often, someone will ask a question which is in fact dealt with slightly later in the pitch. Take advantage of that. Flatter them. Say, 'I'm afraid you're three slides ahead of me: but if you hold on, I'll catch up with you in a second and we can deal with it then.' This is a good device, but make sure that when you do get to the relevant slide, you refer back properly to his question.

The last point on questions relates to your body language when you take a question. It's a mind-blastingly obvious point yet it's forgotten painfully often. When someone asks you a question, *look at them*. Look at them with the rapt attention of a person who is about to be told the map reference for buried treasure, or at least the mobile number of the person in the office you've always fancied. Nothing is more flattering than for their question to be taken seriously, and nothing is more insulting than for it not to be.

Remember, when someone asks you a question, they do not really want to know the answer: what they want to know is that they can have a working relationship with you. How you interact with them is far more important than what you say.

Lastly in body language, there is the question of humour. Pitches are a serious business, but if they become too serious it feels stiff and uncomfortable. Taking a lighter tone relaxes people. You can even be a little bit cheeky, if it is done delicately. It shows that you are not afraid of them. A successful pitch is a dialogue between equals, not a plea from a supplicant to a master.

At the end of the pitch, it's important to know how to close the meeting.

When you are pitching, you want a positive answer there and then. But in the real world, that rarely happens. People want time to reflect and discuss amongst themselves before coming back to you. So the key thing, if you aren't going to get a definite 'yes', is to make sure that you don't get a definite 'no'.

If that looks to be a risk, it's essential to find a way of keeping the dialogue going. Use the discussion at the end of the presentation to identify areas that they are not happy with, and then agree what further work you will do to resolve those problems. Set a date to show that new work and stick to it. Then you're still in the game.

17 The different types of pitch

You're after a new job, and you go to an interview with the person you'll be working for. A week later, they ask you back – it looks as if they want you to do the job, but they also want you to be checked over by their boss.

ARE THESE two interviews the same? After all, it's the same company, it's the same job and it's the same you applying for it.

But the truth is these two interviews could not be more different. Your objective in the first interview is to make your boss want you – to feel excited and positive about you. But by the time you've got to the second interview, it's clear that this job has already been done. You are on a shortlist of one, and the purpose of the second interview is for your new boss to show you to their boss and make sure he or she feels comfortable with you. You no longer have to generate excitement, now you have to generate reassurance.

Your task at the first interview was all about the creation of positives, but your task at the second interview is all about the elimination of negatives. And an interview is just like any other pitch – if you are going to be successful, you need to define very clearly what success looks like for that particular pitch.

A good way to start this process is to ask yourself this question: 'Do I want them to say yes to me, or do I simply want them not to say no?'

People with very long pitch lists (government departments would be a good example) often use the first stage of pitching to weed out the no-hopers. So at that stage, it's important to demonstrate a safe pair of hands. But the next round is likely to be one where the candidates are whittled down to a shortlist. At this point, you have to excite the audience. In short, in the first round you want to avoid a 'no', while in the second round you want to achieve a 'yes'. This may sound obvious in principle, but it's surprising how rarely people think it through in practice. Every pitch has a balance between reassurance and excitement. By defining the kind of pitch you are in, you can then decide whether you want to skew the balance towards excitement or reassurance.

The toughest pitch, in many ways, is an internal presentation – in other words, when you are pitching within a large company, for example, to get approval for your department's annual budget. The reason this pitch is so hard is that if you fail you still have to carry on working with the boss who failed you. When an advertising agency pitches for a huge account, they may fail to win it but at least they can console themselves that they will never have to deal with that company again. But if you fail to sell your annual plan to your boss in a large corporation, you still have to work with him the next day and the next month and the next year. (Although if you fail to sell the following year's plan, the problem of having to deal with him may well be replaced by the problem of not having to deal with him.)

The trick in internal presentations is to cultivate the decision-maker before the actual formal pitch. If the decision-maker is your boss, you're likely to have reasonably good and regular access to him anyway. This makes it easy to sound him out gently on the direction your recommendations are going in, and find out whether he's comfortable with that. If he isn't, you can explore with him where his concerns lie. Do this right, and when the final pitch takes place it will be a foregone conclusion.

Of course, if your boss is smart he will realize what you are up to when you try to pre-sell your proposals to him. But then if your boss is smart, he won't mind at all – on the contrary, he will be pleased that you are trying to make the final pitch a fait accompli. Because in a sense that's what he wants to achieve as well. He will want to demonstrate to his colleagues that his subordinates are serving up the kind of solution he wants; and the last thing people in large corporations like is to be surprised.

So if you are in a large company and you are doing an internal presentation, think of the final pitch less as the event itself and more as the prize-giving afterwards. The real pitch happens more subtly in the weeks beforehand.

In this process you must remember that while you are concerned with what your boss thinks, it's not reciprocal. He doesn't care what you think: he cares what his boss thinks. You can make that work for you.

If you can get your boss to identify what his boss is concerned about, you can then give your boss an answer which is easy for him to sell up to his boss.

Clearly this has to be done with a great deal of tact – the last thing you want to imply to your boss is that you think the real power lies above him. But, handled sensitively, it is the key to a successful pitch in a large corporation. (I keep saying 'him', but of course it might just as easily be 'her'. While the gender may be different, the underlying psychology will be the same.)

Interestingly, people making internal presentations in large organizations don't seem to be filled with quite the same adrenalin rush as people pitching externally, such as an ad agency pitch for a new client. Internal pitches seem to have a lacklustre, almost world-weary, quality about them, as if they are no more than part of the tedious routine of daily office life.

Never fall into that trap. In an internal pitch you are not only pitching for your project, your budget or whatever, you're also pitching to keep your job and to grow your career. You're on parade in front of your bosses in a very vivid way. Even if you don't get agreement to every single proposal, a well-handled, exciting pitch in a large company will enhance your career. It hardly needs adding that an unexciting, poorly handled pitch can destroy your career.

Whereas internal pitches are often tainted by a lack of adrenalin and glamour, advertising agency pitches are often tainted by too much. Advertising pitches are a winner-takes-all game with serious money at stake. This provokes an almost manic desire by the typical agency to put on a special show.

This can be monstrously counter-productive, as there are few things less sexy than someone who is overly eager to please.

An advertising agency client isn't really buying one campaign, because most client/agency partnerships last for several years. No, he is buying a long-term relationship. For this, he wants a partner not a servant. In an agency pitch, exciting ideas are important; but cool-headed, mature people are even more important.

It's the difference between being able to please and being eager to please.

If there is one type of pitch which stretches one's grasp of human psychology – not to mention one's grasp of human frailty – to breaking point, then it is the pitch to a bank. I am thinking particularly of investment banks and private equity houses to whom you might well pitch to get funds for an important new project or to buy another company. At the heart of any big commercial proposition, there must be a big *idea*. So you would like an audience that understands ideas. But what you will get, as opposed to what you would like, is an audience that understands *counting*.

Counting is what bankers do. They don't come from a country inhabited by human beings with human emotions. They come from a very different place called Spreadsheet Land where numbers are what matter. If you can measure it, analyse it, audit it, then in Spreadsheet Land that's good. But if you need an act of imagination rather than an act of arithmetic to grasp the idea, then that's bad.

Show a banker an idea which is old, and he will probably dismiss it on the grounds that it isn't new. But show him an idea which is new, and he will definitely dismiss it on the grounds that it is unproven. And unproven means, 'I can't count it, I can't measure it.'

Because, rather obviously, as you can't measure something which doesn't yet exist, you have to use your judgement.

You think people would find it flattering to be asked to use their judgement, but generally they find it frightening. And if they are bankers, they don't just find it frightening, they find it deep down seriously and fundamentally frightening.

How to deal with these people, who are so long on evaluation and so short on imagination?

First, if you are trying to sell a new idea, dig up as much reassurance from the past as you can. If the idea itself is new and untested, what about the people promoting it? Do they have a track record which would give reassurance? Are there similar concepts that have worked in other countries or at other times? Never forget that you are dealing with people who want to enjoy the benefits of a new idea without taking any of the risk.

Secondly, speak their language – and that means numbers. Sales forecasts, for example, should be very precise with well-quantified justification to support them. Now, you and I know that a sales 'forecast' is just a polite term for an informed guess; but bankers don't care to lend money against a guess, they want to do it against a certainty. (Even if it's a certainty for the future, which is clearly a contradiction in terms.) Bankers equate certainty with numerical precision. So have as much numerical justification for your plan as you can possibly imagine, and some more.

Next remember that bankers are interested in money. People selling ideas are often excited by the idea itself. Indeed, you have to be excited by the idea to sell it with any conviction. But a banker has no interest in an idea as an end in itself, he only has an interest in it as a means to the end of making money. So however enthusiastic you feel about your idea, that enthusiasm needs to be woven into a larger fabric of financial certainty, of investment, of profit, of return on capital.

Finally, even bankers have human emotions. They will hide it well, but they still want to be excited by your new venture. Yes, that little bit of excitement needs to be buried under a ton of reassurance, but nonetheless it must be there. I once saw a very successful businessman pitch to a huge bank for funds for a new and quite risky project. While his pitch was pockmarked with reassurances, spreadsheets and financial analysis, he still radiated huge confidence about the absolute certainty of glorious success in the future. He knew his audience wanted greedy helpings of reassurance (and they got it) but he knew that they also wanted to see a glimpse of stocking top. He made sure they got that too. He got his deal.

Some of the skills in pitching are utterly constant: clarity, confidence, simplicity. But what can vary widely are the needs and nature of your audience. Assess this carefully in advance – are you looking to achieve a 'yes' or simply to avoid a 'no'? All pitches need an element of reassurance and an element of excitement. Where in this spectrum does your particular pitch lie? And what will be the final most important arbiter for your audience? In an advertising agency pitch, it's likely to be the quality of the relationship you offer. In an investment bank pitch, it's likely to be the quantity of money you offer.

You can never offer what your audience wants unless you have first defined exactly what that is.

18 Two's company, three's a committee, or, the art of collaboration

Writing a business presentation, writing a best man's speech at a wedding, writing an after-dinner talk – these are all creative acts. Of course they need structure, as any kind of pitch does.

AND DON'T imagine that a best man's speech is not a pitch: you're pitching to help make a success of what is supposed to be the happiest day of their lives.

Stakes in pitching don't come much higher than that.

Yes, these pitches need structure, as all pitches do. But they also need something far more elusive. They require thought: more specifically they require lateral, rather than vertical, thought. In other words, they need more than organization, they need ideas.

It is the need to generate ideas that defines a creative act. It is also the need to generate ideas that makes us want to retreat underneath the duvet and hide for a day or two. The generation of ideas is a truly scary challenge. That's what writer's block is, after all. It's simply the professional writer's blue funk in the face of having to produce some *ideas*. If it afflicts the professionals that way, it's hardly surprising that it's highly frightening to the rest of us.

Knowing that Marcel Proust had writer's block and knowing that the leader writers at *The Times* suffer from it may give us some comfort, but it doesn't make the problem go away. No, we have to find a way of changing gear out of I-can't-do-this mode and into I'm-getting-on-with-this mode. There is one technique which is hugely helpful in this; and that is to collaborate with someone else.

But be warned: while successful collaboration can be – literally – inspiring, unsuccessful collaboration is much more common. And it is corrosive. A collaboration which doesn't deliver will give you the feeling that you have taken one step forwards and three steps back.

To collaborate successfully, you first need to understand the psychology of vertical and lateral thought. Vertical thinking is logical, organized, connected thinking. It somehow seems correct and proper because it has order to it. Other people can relate to it and understand it: it fits in with the world they already know.

But lateral thinking is anarchic. Looking at things in new ways means, by definition, being willing to challenge taboos and conventional beliefs. An original thinker is someone who has thoughts nobody has had before. How can other people easily relate to that?

Because new ideas aren't comfortable, because they don't fit in with existing concepts (how can they, if they are genuinely original?), they seem like forbidden territory.

That makes them slightly alarming: and it certainly makes the process of inventing them seem alarming. No wonder even professional writers get plagued by writer's block.

The responsibility of producing new, perhaps uncomfortable, ideas is a heavy one. The joy of collaboration is that the responsibility is shared. The pressure is eased. But a level of pressure is still present: and it needs to be, otherwise nothing will happen. You can observe from your own experience how difficult it becomes to produce something when there is no time deadline. The two of you still have the pressure to do it – but at least you do it together.

Note here 'the two of you': if collaboration extends to three or more, the team becomes a committee. The result of this is that most of your time will be spent arguing how the work should be divided between you, not getting on and doing it. Groups of even three, let alone more, start to demand their own hierarchy. Politics creep in; partnership fades out. The strength of two working together is that both know the responsibility is shared. The weakness of three or more working together is that subconsciously each of you is imagining that it's one of the others who is really responsible.

A team of more than two can play a big part in a successful pitch: indeed most successful pitches do involve a larger team. But the part of the task where creativity is paramount, the part of the task *where the ideas are generated*, that part should never be entrusted to more than two of you.

If you need lateral thinking, if you need ideas, avoid the committee and embrace the partnership.

Though recently there have been a few famous partnerships in art, such as Gilbert and George or Jake and Dinos Chapman, it is in comic opera and musicals that the partnership is most often found and most clearly successful. The best examples include Gilbert and Sulllivan, Rodgers and Hammerstein and, latterly, Tim Rice and Andrew Lloyd Webber. The obvious reason for this is that words and music are two different skills, so two different talents are needed. However, partnership goes beyond different skills – it is as much about *differing personalities*.

In advertising it has been usual for many years for a copywriter and an art director to work together. In theory, one has verbal skills, the other has visual skills. In practice, it goes much deeper than that. Writers are usually more structured in their approach to problems; art directors are more lateral. What matters is not that they do different things, but that they do them in different ways.

It's the yin and yang of contrasting temperaments that make a partnership work. After all, if they were too alike, one wouldn't add much to the other. So search for a partner who will surprise you, not support you. You're after challenge, not comfort.

While you're different, it is key to a good creative partnership that you are equal. You're in this thing together.

Like any other marriage, a creative partnership works best when there is time together, but there is also time apart. Work together on debating and understanding the problem, and work together on the road to an answer. But when it comes to spelling out how the solution works, it's just slow and confusing to do it jointly. One of you has to trust the other to set it out.

You can have two people design the car, but you can't both drive it at the same time.

One of the greatest creative partnerships was, of course, Lennon and McCartney. They influenced each other profoundly, but they often developed songs on their own. Many of the songs attributed to both of them were actually written by just one: yet the personality of the other still hovers in the background. That was proved when they stopped writing as a team. Without McCartney's softening touch, Lennon's work often became crudely strident; and without Lennon's attack and edginess, McCartney's work frequently descended into sentimentality.

If you work with someone else, give yourselves the space and time to make the partnership work. When you're together, give the task – and your partner – total concentration. You turn off your mobile when you go to the cinema, so do the same (literally and metaphorically) when you're working with a partner.

If you are working together to find a creative answer to a problem, don't expect it to happen quickly. Creating good ideas is hard enough: doing it to a timetable is almost impossible. The more aware of the clock you are, the more certain you are to suffer a kind of constipation of the imagination.

Hide from the rest of the world; forget the deadline; and enjoy each other's company. Good things happen when you don't press too hard.

Above all, encourage each other, and make the work fun. The whole point of a collaboration is that you move from the world of 'I can't do it' to the world of 'We can do it'.

19 The loneliness of power

From the outside, being Chief Executive of a business looks pretty good – the chauffeur-driven car, the large salary, the deference you get from others.

IT FEELS very different from the inside looking out. The large salary soon gets taken up with large outgoings: it's scary how quickly you expand your spending to match your earning. The deference of others counts for little, as you realize it's rooted not in respect but in fear. And while the chauffeur is a nice luxury (especially in the week before Christmas, when he saves you a fortune in parking tickets), his very existence deprives you of the last shreds of privacy. And he'll end up knowing more about your private life than is healthy for any employee.

No, the truth is that a Chief Executive is trapped between pressure from beneath and pressure from above.

The pressure from beneath comes from employees who want more money, more bonuses, more promotions. They expect him to accept all their advice and yet to exercise strong leadership himself – a contradiction if ever there was one.

The painful truth is that the Chief Executive can trust no one beneath him. They will all promise loyalty whilst secretly hoping for his downfall, to create a gap for them to fill.

While the CEO has to deal with these pressures from below, he will have shareholders and a board above him who place the whole burden of success on his shoulders and no one else's. They will expect him to carry the can for failure, and conveniently forget that it was their own unreasonable demands, lack of vision and slowness to decide that caused the problem in the first place. It's just human nature, given a choice between blaming yourself and blaming someone else, to decide that it's someone else who has to go.

> **In short, a Chief Executive is a lonely figure. In public, he'll put a brave face on it, but in private, he is isolated.**

He has pressures from above and from below; he has a lot to lose; and he has no one to share that with.

And that is where the opportunity lies: *he has no one to share that with*.

If you are pitching to a large company as an adviser – be it advertising agency, investment bank, PR consultancy, whatever – you have a unique opportunity to be that lonely CEO's one true friend. As we have seen, he simply won't trust any of the people under him, since the bright ones will be after his job. He can hardly confide in his shareholders about his problems, as they are only interested in his solutions. He will fear, quite rightly, that shareholders would see such confiding as a sign of weakness.

But he can talk to you. Unlike the shareholders, you don't have the power to take his job away. Unlike his staff, you don't want his job for yourself. Indeed you too may well be a lonely CEO. Who better to share confidences and anxieties with?

But most pitchers blow this great opportunity. Why? How?

The CEO to whom you are pitching will, subconsciously, be looking for a friend as well as a solution. What characterizes friendships? It's certainly not that the two people are alike in temperament – often the best friendships are based on the attraction of opposites. But while they may not be alike, they always treat each other as equals.

So, when you pitch to your CEO, he must see you as his equal. If not, you can never be his friend, his confidant. This is where so many pitchers blow the opportunity to forge a 'special relationship'.

They blow it by wanting the contract too much, by being too subservient. They behave like servants, not like partners. You must show the confidence which establishes you as an equal. (That doesn't mean you're cocky: a false over-confidence is about the least confidence-inspiring posture known to man.) No, you're just naturally confident. You're running your business; he's running his. Don't be fazed by the fact that his business is a huge corporation and yours is John Smith and Partners: you're both facing exactly the same kind of pressure – from above and below – and if you can help him share those pressures rather than dwell on them in lonely isolation, you have an ally for life.

And believe me, in business, Chief Executives are the best kind of ally to have. Because with them is where the power lies.

20 Numbers, nervousness and nonsense; or, the role of management consultants in a civilized society

Presentations in business are often triggered by a big strategic question, such as how to reposition a tired brand or how to evaluate a large investment decision. When strategic choices are in the air, sooner or later someone is going to suggest bringing in management consultants.

'WHY DON'T we get McKinsey to have a look at it?' goes the cry. Indeed, why don't we? After all, the ancient Romans, when faced with a big and difficult choice, would seek help from a soothsayer. He would kill a few chickens, hurl their entrails around in an apparently random fashion, and then give his verdict. Amazingly, the Romans (who were smart enough to build one of the greatest empires in history) would go off satisfied. The ancient Greeks, when facing a similar choice, would go to Delphi and consult the resident charlatan – or 'oracle' as he was then called – listen to an utterly spurious answer and go away satisfied.

Yes, that's the same ancient Greeks who gave us the foundations of modern thought and philosophy.

So some really bright peoples have relied on some really meretricious nonsense when they wanted comfort from the lonely feeling that envelops us all when a big decision has to be made. That hasn't changed; the only difference is that we don't say 'soothsayers' any more, we call them Management Consultants.

'Ah, yes,' I hear you say, 'but consultants are rather more sophisticated: they don't rely on chicken innards in their business-planning models. They are clever people: why shouldn't we use them?'

The first, and often strongest, argument against consultants is their high cost. And they certainly are expensive. A smaller consultancy job will result in an invoice for a six-figure amount, and when they get going, invoices in the millions are normal.

Paradoxically, this is the one criticism of consultants I don't accept. If they truly can solve a major business problem, a fee of a million pounds may be a very good investment.

The question is not: 'Was the medicine expensive?'

The question is: 'Did the medicine work?'

Clearly, some folk think consultants do deliver, otherwise they wouldn't still be in business. They certainly wouldn't be in business in the grand style that many of them now are. What is it that people see in consultants?

Presumably, they think that consultants will solve their problem: often a problem which will otherwise get filed under 'too difficult'. But why do they believe these outsiders will solve something even the insiders can't do? There are three virtues that consultants are supposed to bring to bear on your business problem:

- They are objective: not being bogged down in the day-by-day detail of the business, they can give you fresh thinking.
- They look at lots of different businesses, so they have a much broader knowledge of what works and what doesn't.
- They are scarily clever.

What is the truth in this?

They genuinely are objective. So far, so good.

They do look at a wide range of businesses – but do they really understand them? Consultants make their recommendations and move on. They don't live long enough with the businesses they advise to know how those ideas have worked in practice. They look at business in theory, *but they are not the ones responsible for delivering anything in practice*.

> This begs a question: would you take lessons in life-saving from someone who'd learnt to swim on dry land?

At least they are very clever – or so it is routinely assumed.

The sad truth about consultants, however, is that they are often clever but they are rarely wise.

The distinction between being clever and being wise gets to the heart of what's wrong with management consultants. Someone who is merely clever impresses with his knowledge; someone who is wise does the right thing.

McKinsey himself gave us a tragically clear insight into this distinction when he said, 'Everything can be measured and what gets measured gets managed.'

Few statements can be more superficially clever than this; and few statements – when examined with a little thought – could be more blisteringly stupid.

Try telling a doctor dealing with the terminally ill that if you can measure it you can manage it. Yes, he can measure the patients' pulse, temperature and a whole lot more. Problem is, he can't stop them dying. We can measure the point when, on current trends, the world will run out of oil. But do we then stop driving our cars? Or take our holiday at home to save aviation fuel?

McKinsey's remark sums up, in one little sentence, so much that is wrong not just with management consultants but with the whole way business is understood. There is an underlying assumption that it's all about measurement and numbers. It isn't. Numbers may be how you keep the score, but they aren't how you play the game.

What drives business success is emotion: passion, greed, ambition, determination, courage.

It takes courage to take a risk – not numbers. It takes determination to build a business – not numbers. It takes passion to keep going when lesser mortals would cave in – not numbers. It takes imagination to create a new idea which changes a market – not numbers. It takes inspiration to motivate staff through a difficult time – not numbers.

When we interviewed Sir Gerry Robinson for this book he said, 'People think it's all done through the numbers; that's how business works. They think that somehow emotions don't come into it and it's all done in a kind of vacuum. But actually most good decisions are made emotionally.'

Obviously numbers matter, because that's how you evaluate achievement. But it is not how you create achievement. You need a stopwatch in the Olympics to evaluate the runners: but it's the athletes who win the gold medals, not the timekeepers.

If you and I can grasp this simple point, why can't McKinsey?

It's all to do with the temperament of people who choose to be management consultants in the first place. They are, intellectually, bright. But emotionally they are voyeurs not participants in life's bordello. They can observe and they can comment. But they can't do it. They can tell you how, but they can't take responsibility themselves. They are serial offerers of opinion, but they are also serial avoiders of responsibility.

After all, if they could take responsibility for a large business – rather than telling someone else how to do it – don't you think they would? But it's not right to blame the politicians without putting some of the blame on the voters who elected them. By the same token, we can't blame consultants and yet excuse the clients who hired them. It's instructive to look at the kind of organizations who use consultants most.

Yes, you guessed it, the main users of consultants are large corporations and government. In other words, bureaucracies, places where process matters more than performance, where people want comfort not challenge.

In contrast, the kind of organizations where fast growth happens, where ideas flourish, where originality is valued – do you see many of them on the client list at McKinsey or Bain? Hardly.

The moral is simple. If you can do it, then do it. If you can't do it, then learn how to do it. But don't put your trust in someone who tells others how to, but never has himself.

21 The interview: the most personal of pitches

All pitches are a personal test. But they are not a test of you alone. They may be a test of you and your team; they may be a test of you and your idea; they may be a test of you and your company's reputation. You are important, but you are not carrying the weight entirely on your own.

EXCEPT IN one very special case: the interview. When you are being interviewed for a job, then you are in the dock utterly alone.

Of course, an interview is scary because there's usually a lot at stake. Will you get the job you want, which might define the next five or ten years of your life? That's frightening enough, but it's made much worse by your isolation. It's about you, and nothing else.

Given that it's such a big test, it's better to be well prepared for it. That starts with your CV. Without a good CV you may well never get there. Even if you do, your CV will be used as a prompt by the interviewer, so if it's not exceptional the interview starts on the back foot.

Most people think a good CV depends on a career of achievement; it's all about what you've done, not how you set it out. That's only half the story. A badly set-out CV (and believe me, that is most of them) can make good achievement look boring; while a good CV becomes an achievement in its own right.

So what constitutes a good CV?

First, make it short. Very short. The people reading your CV are not only reading yours; they may well be reading fifty more. Be merciful to them. You may be interested in the fact that you won the under-16 athletics at St Cake's, but they won't be. The less you say about the jobs you've done, the more you'll have to talk about when you meet. And don't think that having the shortest CV will draw attention to you in a bad way; the opposite is true.

Second, think what the new job is, think what you have done, and find ways to link them. Highlight the experiences you have had that will be relevant to them.

Third, analyse your strengths and weaknesses, then find ways to overcome the weak points and emphasize the good. For example, if you have done junior jobs in big companies, lay out the jobs by the name of the companies, not your role. This sounds obvious, but how many people really revise their CV in this way for each new opportunity?

Fourth, show your personality. A graduate I know well wanted a career in film, but had no relevant experience. In his CV he put a section headed: 'Relevant Experience'.

Underneath, he wrote:

'Absolutely none whatsoever.
But I work hard
I'll take on any task
I'll work for virtually nothing
and I make a blinding cup of tea.'

He got the job and is now a successful film director.

Follow his example; don't be afraid to ignore the conventional format in order to show your own character better.

Fifth, don't say anything about your private life unless you can make it interesting. You may well be married with two children, have a house in the suburbs, and enjoy the odd game of golf. There's nothing wrong with that – until you put it in a CV. Then it becomes boring. Forget the golf and invent some much more esoteric hobby, like mountaineering or underwater photography. Obviously you'll need to study the subject a bit before the interview, in case you find yourself being cross-examined by a keen weekend mountaineer. Even then, you can confess to being a beginner. It still beats golf, and they'll be reassured to know they are better at mountaineering than you are.

Sixth, get a designer to help you make it look distinctive. Even now, when most CVs are sent electronically, there are things you can do to the type, the layout, the spacing, to make your document look special.

Lastly, don't be embarrassed to include a photo of yourself. You'd be surprised how easy it is, when twenty candidates are interviewed over three or four weeks, for the interviewer to forget which one is which. You are far more likely to be chosen for the next round if you are easily identified.

Because CVs follow a standard format, they tend to make all candidates look the same: an irony, given that their whole purpose is to show how you are different. So keep it short, keep it to the point, and try to impose your personality on it in some way.

Now we've got a CV that's strong, how do we handle the interview itself?

The underlying strategy is the same as for any successful pitch: it's about simplicity, it's about confidence, and above all it's about *them* as well as *you*.

Start by doing some research on the company that is interviewing you. If it's Marks & Spencer, visit some shops; if it's BMW, test drive a car. If the headquarters and the interview are in London, the next time you're visiting friends in the country, find time to visit some of the company's out of town premises. Above all, get hold of the annual report and read it from cover to cover. There's always something in it you can refer to in the interview. What's important is to demonstrate that you have really done some homework on their business. It flatters them; it shows you've made an effort; and above all it makes the point that you are interested in what you can do for them, not what they can do for you.

Analyse – as you did with your CV – your particular strengths and weaknesses for this job. Find a good and simple counter-argument for the weaknesses. If you are too young, stress your enthusiasm and inexpensiveness; if you are too old, stress your experience. Similarly, find ways of focusing on your good points, particularly your relevant experience. There is risk in employing anyone, and relevant experience will greatly reduce that risk in the minds of your inquisitors.

If you find you don't have relevant experience, don't stop looking. You may not have worked in a similar company, but have you faced a similar problem? Think a little laterally about this if you need to; and remember that they crave the reassurance that you can do it for them because you've done it before.

You are not only selling to them; they are selling the job to you. Without being aggressive, they need to sense that you know that. Prepare a sensible list of questions about the job and about the company. People love talking about themselves and their business (much more fun than finding out about you), so let them. Don't be shy about referring overtly to your pre-planned list of questions – it shows you've come prepared and that you want to learn about them. If you get them talking, it's been a good interview. And if they start selling the job to you, it becomes a dialogue between equals that puts you in a much more confident position.

Make your answers short and uncomplicated. Rehearse your response to some obvious questions in advance, so you can achieve this. There's a huge temptation to go into a long monologue about what you've done. Don't. It's boring. Keep it simple; and if that leaves them wanting more, so much the better.

The magic of striving for brevity is that it forces you to sweep aside the small print and focus on the big strategic issues. That way, you capture the high ground.

Finally, when the interview is over, it isn't. The job is not done when you leave the room.

Write them a friendly, short note of thanks for seeing you, and make sure it's in the post the very next day. It has to be a letter, not an e-mail, because letters are far rarer and much nicer to receive. Then call a few days later with a couple of sensible questions. Why? Because hardly anybody else will. Interest flatters; your feedback tells the interviewers that they have done a good job because they have inspired a dialogue. And it sets you apart.

22 What have we learnt?

Let's take stock of what we've learnt: what does a battle-plan for a great pitch look like?

BEGIN BY understanding how crucial the pitch is. In life's transactions, the pitch is where decisions are made.

Then remember that pitching is a theatre where the potency of emotions counts for far, far more than the aridity of statistics, information and analysis.

To capture those emotions, you must write a great pitch before you can deliver a great pitch: the playwright's role comes before the actor's.

To be a successful playwright, you must ruthlessly set aside enough time (or more than enough) and find a place which insulates you from other pressures and distractions.

Shape your pitch from the foundations up – get the big ideas in place first, and worry about details later.

Give your argument structure – set up your proposition, develop it, summarize it.

Let your argument explore and understand the problems first: only then do you move to defining a solution. Articulate your answer as simply as you dare. Cut away the fat and never forget that your audience want one big answer, not fifteen little ones. (And remember that there is no such thing as an utterly perfect solution: the best available practical answer is the winner.)

Find one sentence, one slide, on which your argument hinges. That will make you think more simply and your story will be much easier to grasp.

Summarize at the end, never at the beginning. Sales of detective novels would be slow if the first chapter always told you the ending.

Use PowerPoint if you want, but don't let it use you. Draft your pitch using pencil and paper before even switching on your laptop.

Rehearse with colleagues to get the content right; rehearse on your own to get delivery right. And burn those notes – you are *pitching*, not reading out loud.

Above all, trust your own instincts and radiate confidence. They are buying you as much as your solution, and if you believe in yourself there's every chance they will too.

Like all the big things in life, a pitch seems hard when you're worrying about it in advance, but it falls into place as soon as you start to deal with it.

Now you can do it – yet if you want to be not just a good presenter but an excellent one, you need to think and learn about the underlying psychology of the pitch . . .

23 The psychology of pitching – understanding the transfer of power

To pitch brilliantly, you need to sense what is going on beneath the surface. You must grasp the psychology which underlies every pitch.

IN TRUTH that psychology is simple: a pitch is an attempt to transfer power from the audience to the pitcher. You pitch to an investment bank for funding for a new business; they have the power to give you the money you need to launch your business. And they have the power to reject you.

You pitch to Guinness for their advertising account; they have the power to give you that business and make your advertising agency more successful overnight. Even a date is about the transfer of power – does she want to yield to him, surrendering herself and surrendering her power?

So the audience for a pitch has the power: the power to give you money; the power to give you sex; the power to give you opportunity. Not unnaturally, people with power are reluctant to give it up. The easiest course is always to say 'no'.

The shrewd pitcher deals with that at two levels. He must defuse the angst of giving away power; he must deal with his audience's fear of loss and risk. He needs to reassure them, to minimize risk, to make it safe to say 'yes'.

But at the same time he must excite them: no one is going to concede power unless they get something in return. He must offer them something which will make them *want* to say 'yes'.

It's about the removal of negatives and the creation of positives. It's about a subtle intertwining of reassurance and excitement. The shrewd advertising agency pitching for Guinness will excite the team from the brewery with the bait that their advertising idea – thanks to its originality, relevance, etc. – will drive sales up. But they will also reassure them that nothing can go wrong – we've researched the idea thoroughly so we know it's going to work, we're safe because we've worked in the drinks market for years, etc. And a man inviting a woman to a restaurant with his mind set more on lust than on lunch will seek to excite her with implications of the good time they could share. But he may also seek to reassure her that the liaison he proposes will have depth and commitment – he is attracted by her beautiful nature as much as by her beautiful legs.

This balance between excitement and reassurance was demonstrated wonderfully by a story Sir Gerry Robinson told me. Gerry is most famous for his astonishing business career and then his television series as a business guru. But it was his role as Chairman of the Arts Council which led to this fascinating insight into the art of pitching.

Gerry was chosen to run the Arts Council because the government of the day (led by Tony Blair as Prime Minister and Gordon Brown as Chancellor) thought the Council was badly and extravagantly managed. So they wanted a hard-headed businessman to get hold of it and cut the waste. But when Gerry studied it, he quickly decided the arts needed more money, not less. I asked him how he pitched this exceptionally difficult case to the very people who had put him in place to recommend the opposite. His answer was revealing:

> 'We had to get to the right people to get the message across. If I had asked for more money at the Department of Culture, I just wouldn't have got it. I completely bypassed them and talked direct to Gordon Brown and Tony Blair.
>
> 'I had to point out that the problems weren't just inefficiencies, although there was some of that, but the arts were just ludicrously underfunded. Any civilized nation should fund the arts properly. I felt that it was a credible proposition for me to be saying that, rather than someone from the arts world.'

I asked Gerry what was his clinching argument, and he replied,

> 'I just knew that the way to get the money was to point out that what was needed, £200 million, was in real terms absolutely bugger all. I reminded them it was just about the cost of one F-11 jet.'

Getting £200 million out of a tough Scottish chancellor and his Prime Minister is a hard task, yet Gerry makes it all seem so easy, doesn't he?

But Gerry played every move perfectly. He went straight to the top for his decision, to the people who had the power to say 'yes'. He traded on his reputation as a businessman who's tough on money. He presented his case simply. What Prime Minister, faced with 'every civilized nation funds its arts properly' would want to categorize his nation as uncivilized?

Finally, he made the decision seem small, unremarkable, risk-free: '...absolutely bugger all, the cost of one F-11 jet'. Brilliant. No wonder Gerry could just about afford his own F-11 if he wanted to.

This is a perfect example of how to stress the positive (being a civilized nation, doing things properly) while skilfully eliminating the negative by making the high cost magically disappear into an aircraft hangar somewhere.

> We've observed how a pitch is a delicately balanced framework of vulnerability and power. But don't make the mistake of thinking that the power is all on one side, and the vulnerability is all on the other.

Your advertising agency wants the Guinness account more than life itself – but the people at Guinness want effective advertising. More than that, in a large corporation, they also want to be seen to have made the right decision.

So they have something you want, but you have something they want. And that applies in every pitch – you may be pitching to them, but in a sense they are pitching to you. When you ask a bank to fund your business, they want to be sure your idea is good before they get their cheque-book out. But they also want to be sure that you don't take your good idea to another bank.

The job interview is another good example of this. When you go for the interview, you are only interested in whether they offer you the job: but while you need the job, they need the job vacancy filled. So they have to sell the job to you, as you have to sell yourself to them.

Understanding that the transfer of power in a pitch is a two-way street is massively important. Of course, they have something you want. But never forget that you have something they want. Because then you will come across far more confidently. It has become a discussion between equals. And as we have seen before, your confidence in a pitch is the most powerful weapon you can have.

24 The business of living – Al Capone, the Queen, and how they connect

We've talked about pitching and its role in business; but what about its role in the business of living? The truth is that lessons you can learn about business have an equally powerful application to life in a broader sense, because business is a metaphor for life – all the battles, anxieties and triumphs you'll meet in business are echoed, often more loudly, in the business of life.

TO UNDERSTAND why this is, you only have to look at how business is structured and then see how closely that mirrors the way society is structured. The central component in the structure of society is the family. In a primitive society, the tribe is simply a grouping of families: and in modern society, a nation is simply a tribe on a huge scale.

Now look at the business world and observe how each company is also shaped like a family. The Chief Executive is the father figure; responsible for both leadership and discipline, as well as the ultimate decision-maker. The softer, more nurturing tasks in a company fall to the mother figure, the HR director. (A quick check of the boards of leading UK companies shows that a surprisingly large number of HR directors are women.) And a company behaves just like a family: when there is pressure from outside, everyone sticks together, but when there is not, there is any amount of petty in-fighting and rivalry.

You can find interesting confirmation of this in language. Just about the most powerful and rich (not to mention ruthless) business group in the world is the Mafia – who call each of their companies a family. At a rather different position in the social scale, one of the richest and perhaps most influential families in the world is the British royal family. How do they describe themselves when talking to each other? The members of the royal family call themselves 'the firm'.

There's a delicious irony that the Mafia call a firm a family while the royals call their family a firm. Al Capone and Queen Elizabeth II agree on at least one thing – the language they use shows they both see the analogy between business and family life: the family and the firm mirror each other uncannily closely.

At the heart of how business is structured is the organization of power and responsibility. The very shape of a business is there to determine who is in charge of what and who reports to whom. In the other complex structures we have created – universities, government, the judiciary – the recurring theme is that each structure is centred on a plan for the management of power and responsibility. But at the heart of family life we also find the organization of power and responsibility: who is in charge of earning, who is in charge of cooking and the home, how is responsibility for the children to be shared? Any psychologist will confirm the parallels between the business unit and the family unit by telling you that employees who have an unusually combative relationship with their boss have, almost inevitably, had a similarly combative relationship with their father. As it was with the father, so it is later with the father figure.

This becomes significant when we see how lessons learnt in business can be applied on a broader basis to our life in society. If you can get it right at the office, you can get it right everywhere.

25 Life: a non-stop pitch

It's easy to imagine that pitches happen at the office and nowhere else. Easy, but wrong – and dangerously so.

OF COURSE we know when pitches happen at work. The big crunch meeting is put in the diary a month in advance. Everyone knows about it, everyone agonizes about it. Or so it seems.

Actually we are endlessly engaged in pitches at work that we often fail to recognize as pitches at all. Let's agree that a pitch is a moment when you have a chance to present your case, and so present yourself. On that basis, your monthly review with your boss is a pitch. We can agree on that. What about the day you spend travelling with him, and you're together for two hours at the airport and two more in the plane?

Well, it may not seem a pitch to you, but he has the opportunity (a very long opportunity, as it happens) to study you, to talk to you about stuff you don't get to talk about in the office, to be entertained by you, to be bored by you. That's not a pitch? If he could end the day feeling somewhat differently about you, then that was a pitch all right.

Of course the big formal moments are the obvious pitch moments, because they are planned as a pitch and because a decision is expected. But don't underestimate the significance of the normal everyday encounters. If they shape how people see you – and they do – they can carry all the power of a pitch even though they don't carry the name. One of those everyday encounters may not shape an opinion, but the cumulative effect of two or three certainly will.

The painful truth is that, at work, we're on trial all the time.

And if it's true that we're always on trial at work, it's even more true in our lives outside work. Our working life is relatively structured, and our work diaries are peppered with meetings, reviews, conferences, events. Each of these gives us the opportunity to pitch our case. But outside work, our life is much less structured and many social encounters are more spontaneous. In these situations, pitching becomes much less about how you present your case and much more about how you present yourself. That doesn't make it any less important. Life outside work is filled with moments when how you present yourself is crucial – parent/teacher evenings, dinner parties, as a host at home, on a date.

All of these moments matter. How you behave at a social event will have a real bearing on the invitations you receive, the esteem you are held in, the friendships you develop. How you behave on a date may determine whether it leads to a painful jolt of disappointment or a long and wondrous love affair.

The significance of how you present yourself on a date is well understood in nature: just look at the plumage of a cock pheasant, with his magnificent array of green, black, violet and white head feathers. The hen pheasant, meanwhile, has a dull buff and brown plumage, described in one bird guide as 'rather nondescript'. In short, the hen pheasant is the audience in life's mating game while the cock is the pitcher: he has to sell himself to her, and he is always dressed for the occasion. She simply has to choose which pitch pleases her the best.

So we don't just pitch at work: the whole of life is a non-stop pitch. How do we deal with that, when we don't take a PowerPoint presentation to a parent/teacher evening and we can't rehearse our witty repartee before a dinner party?

Surprisingly perhaps, many of the same lessons which apply in business also apply in life. You need to understand your audience and to be a good listener. You need to be confident and to learn how to express yourself quickly and simply. Get these things right and you develop your own personal brand of charm. And having charm is a bit like learning to drive a car: you have to concentrate ferociously at first, but gradually it becomes natural, something you do without needing to think about it.

But when do you need to apply that charm? We've seen how in office life the formal pitch is punctuated by many much briefer and more spontaneous encounters, each of which is still a pitch – in the crucial sense that your performance can be judged by others. At each of these encounters, your audience is taking a new snapshot of you and how you present yourself. And like a photographic snapshot, the image is formed instantaneously but the impression it creates can last for ever. If it doesn't last for ever, it's only because a newer snapshot has been taken since, which updates the impression of you. So business life has a small number of big Pitches, with a capital 'P', but in between there are any number of small 'p' pitches – those encounters where a snapshot view of you is taken.

Life outside the office is no different – you are subject to obvious scrutiny on the big occasions, but you are also subject to continuing scrutiny at every snapshot moment.

26 The snapshot moment

The capital 'P' Pitches in life are easy to identify. We've mentioned a parent/teacher evening as one example, and another is the date which could lead to a passionate affair – or to a lonely and disappointed taxi ride home. But what about those snapshot moments which are less obvious? How do we recognize them? And how do we deal with them?

THINK ABOUT that date for a second: let's imagine it does lead to a big romance, and a lasting relationship. Don't imagine that your pitching is over. On the contrary, a lasting relationship has to be nurtured. It offers an unending series of snapshot moments, where your partner can update the image of you they carry in their heart. How do you show sympathy when your partner is ill, or has a problem to cope with? When you both have good news on the same day, do you tell your partner all about your news, or do you let them tell you about theirs first?

We've all heard that old cliché 'You've got to work at a marriage' a thousand times. But don't dismiss it just because it's timeworn. It's a reminder that once you've won the big pitch – getting married – you still have to deal with the endless small pitches of keeping romance vibrant in the face of routine. The chilling thing about these small pitches, the snapshot moments, is that the negative snapshot leaves a much more enduring memory than the positive snapshot. A kind word and a kiss are quickly forgotten, but even a small row can smoulder on for ages.

> Like a good stew, a row increases in intensity of flavour if you leave it overnight and reheat it. So the positive moments have to be truly positive if they are to have staying power.

A car needs fuel, cleaning, maintenance, running repairs. So does a relationship. Don't wait for a snapshot moment to happen; if you do, chances are that it will be a bad moment not a good one. Of course, a birthday or a wedding anniversary offers you a snapshot moment; but relationships need care and attention far more frequently than once or twice a year.

In a relationship you can't be perfect all the time, but you need to create moments when you both remember why you fell in love in the first place.

In a continuing relationship, it shouldn't be too hard to create those special snapshots because you know what your partner particularly likes and enjoys. It's harder in a social encounter, a dinner party for example, where you may be meeting people you don't know. The key is to drop your ambition to be known as a good talker, and embrace the ambition of being known as a good listener instead.

Don't tell them about yourself; ask them about themselves. Ask them about their children; or if they're younger, about their boyfriend or girlfriend.

> Research in America has shown that in social meetings the people who listened most were regarded by the others as the best conversationalists.

If there is something you want them to know about you, don't tell them but let them find it out. People prefer to discover, rather than to be shown. And think about what it is you want them to discover. Your achievements may be achievements to you, but they may well be pure boredom to others. Far better to let them find out about your insecurities, your vulnerabilities.

Why should your vulnerabilities be more attractive than your victories? There's a curious reverse psychology at work here. We've talked a number of times about the importance of confidence, and about the power it gives to the pitcher. Paradoxically, revealing your weaknesses shows far more confidence than revealing your strengths. Anyone can boast about what they have got right: to talk about what you have got wrong takes real courage. And showing courage inspires confidence.

So it's clear that throughout life we are endlessly presenting ourselves to be captured in a snapshot moment; and that snapshot can leave a lasting impression. In a relationship we need, quite deliberately, to create those moments in order to keep the relationship strong, fresh and exciting. In other encounters, the snapshot will be positive if we are good listeners – we must provoke discussion not dominate it. And when we do get drawn into discussion, the trick is not to show ourselves too much to others but to let them discover us. And if the 'us' they discover has the courage to reveal weakness, we emerge all the stronger for it.

Yet all this stuff about listening, about not imposing yourself, about not hiding weakness: it all sounds like a formula for coming across as a personality which is likeable but somehow not very muscular. Don't we need to find some other, more positive way of defining ourselves to the rest of the world?

Yes, we do – and this is where charisma becomes important.

27 Charisma, or, the courage to be different

Certain people, when they are presenting their case or presenting themselves, seem to have the battle won before it's fought, because they have that elusive quality we call charisma. Charisma appears to be a very special gift that's easy to recognize in others yet dauntingly hard to inculcate in oneself. But the title of this chapter tells you almost all you need to know – because really the magic power of charisma is rooted firmly in having the courage to be a bit different from all the rest.

WHAT DO we really mean by charisma, however? It's a way of being that radiates a particular sense of excitement and magnetism that occurs apparently regardless of what one says or does. People with charisma seem to fill a room without having to do anything more than just be there. They have a natural air of both authority and appeal that doesn't need to be stated, yet is so powerful it's almost palpable.

People with charisma always have a huge sense of self-belief: they behave as if they can deal with anything fate can throw at them. Paradoxically, charismatic people are also able to show great faith in others, and this willingness to trust others can be inspiring. Tim Bell (now Lord Bell) was a close adviser to Margaret Thatcher when she was Prime Minister and told me this story about her.

> 'She was a very special person. Her view was that you are the expert, that's what I've hired you for; so I'll do what you tell me to do. Don't ask me to tell you what you should be doing, I've hired you to do it. She gave you all the responsibility in your area, but in return she expected you to let her get on with her job. Otherwise you got handbagged: if you said something like "I think we should reduce taxes," she would just say, "And who elected you?"'

Charisma has the curious quality of being something you can sense but you can't see. But while it's not visible, it is certainly vivid. You know when someone has it. Indeed it almost seems as if the only way to define it is to identify who has it. Perhaps the most famously charismatic figure in recent times is Che Guevara. Visitors to Cuba will be stunned to see that famous face, sculpted in metal, covering all of a building several storeys high that dominates Havana's main square. This was a face that launched far more than a thousand T-shirts; it launched the concept of liberty against oppression to a generation, not just in Cuba but across the world.

Che Guevara had every ingredient of charisma: he stood for an ideal; he fought for freedom; he won; he was handsome. He even died young, which seems sadly to make the graduation to legendary status much more certain. James Dean and Marilyn Monroe are two tragic but potent examples.

So is that it? All you have to do is be a handsome idealist who dies young? It might seem so, if Che is the only example we take. But what of Che's partner in revolution, Fidel Castro? He certainly had huge charisma, but you'd never accuse him of having Che's film-star looks. What he did have was a sheer force of personality that propelled him to power in Cuba, and kept him there for half a century.

Another great political leader was Winston Churchill, who like Castro lived a long life, and like Castro was not handsome. Of course his achievements as a war leader were astonishing, but his charisma was firmly in place before then. Indeed, it was his charisma which made his war leadership so effective. After the war he was replaced by Attlee, who was arguably the dullest and least charismatic figure in our recent political history. Yet it was Attlee who almost single-handedly created the modern welfare state, the most important achievement in peacetime politics in the last century. Whatever charisma is, Churchill had it and Attlee didn't, so it isn't just to do with achievement. It's to do with *how you are*.

Amongst current world figures, Bill Gates ought to have it: a man whose business has changed all our lives and who happens to be the richest man in the world. Surely that's enough? It should be, but it isn't. Bill Gates may have Microsoft and he may have millions (I should say billions) but he is a charisma-free zone. In the UK Prince Charles should have it, since he's heir to the British throne, has a vast personal fortune, and has managed to be married to a woman of staggering beauty and yet keep a mistress at the same time. But sadly, Charles has about as much charisma as a tax return or a final reminder from the gas board.

In the arts, charisma is rarely found among writers: we all loved Catch 22 but how many of us can even remember what Joseph Heller looks like? But amongst artists, it's less rare. Salvador Dalí oozed charisma, even though he was a money-obsessed, sexually unfulfilled old rogue. But fellow surrealist Magritte – whose work certainly stands comparison with that of Dali – just hasn't got it. Similarly, the anaemic-looking and insecure Andy Warhol had it, but his equally talented pop art contemporaries Lichtenstein and Rauschenberg aren't on the radar. Picasso had it enormously; while Georges Braque who invented Cubism with Picasso . . . well, would you recognize a photograph of Braque?

If we look at those special people who do have this magic gift, we see they come in all shapes and sizes, but they do always seem to have two particular characteristics. First, they aren't afraid to be different from the rest of us. And second, but very important, they look as if they are enjoying themselves. Let's explore those two talents – which I firmly believe they are – a little deeper.

We'll start with being different. Salvador Dalí was about as different as can be, with his waxed moustache, absurd posturing and pseudo-philosophical artspeak. We wouldn't dare; but he did, and that's the secret.

Picasso and Warhol were both different from all around them too. Picasso not only produced a huge body of highly original work, he lived a life of flamboyant self-indulgence in which each new mistress (and there were many) inspired a new direction in his painting. Warhol stood a thousand years of art history on its head by deliberately mass-producing his work – who else would call his studio 'the factory'?

Winston Churchill certainly had no fear of being different. He endlessly smoked huge cigars; slept all morning, then worked through the night; dictated crucial war correspondence to his secretary while lying in the bath; and drank more champagne in a week than most of us do in a lifetime. (This provoked the rebuke from fellow MP Bessie Braddock, 'Mr Churchill, you are drunk.' He famously replied, 'Indeed, madam, and you are ugly, but tomorrow I shall be sober.')

As for Che Guevara and Fidel Castro, they ganged together with about half a dozen friends and liberated Cuba from the USA, the most powerful nation in the world. You don't get much more different or individualistic than that.

All of these extraordinary people had the courage to be different. *They behaved as they wished, not as society expected.* Therein lies their charisma. We would all like to do what we want, not what is expected of us; but we just don't quite have the nerve to go ahead. Ultimately, we conform. People with charisma follow their own path.

And they have fun doing it. That is the other secret to charisma – enjoy what you are doing. Whether or not others enjoyed Salvador Dalí's play-acting, there is no doubt that it gave *him* huge pleasure. Similarly, Warhol loved being at the centre of the attention he generated around himself. Even Churchill, at the worst of the war years, seemed like a man who relished the challenge; and the worse it became the stronger he got. In more recent political times, Bill Clinton, a man of great charisma, always looked to be in charge and enjoying himself, even when things were against him. George Bush in contrast (don't ask which one; they're each as bad as the other, and the point is true of either) looks strained and joyless.

Clearly, you can't just buy a bottle of champagne and a box of cigars and become Churchill, nor will a waxed moustache and a mad self-regard turn you into Dalí. But while you can't imitate charisma, you can learn from it.

What these extraordinary people can all show us is that their self-belief was so great that they were happy to go where their instincts took them, not where convention wanted them to go.

28 The limits of logic, the power of passion

If you ask any number of people whether they thought the word 'reasonable' was a compliment or a criticism, I'd bet that all would see it as a compliment. Probably so would you.

INDEED, VIRTUALLY all of current business practice is based on logic, which is little more than reasonableness developed into a science. Management consultants (remember, they were the ones that learnt to swim on dry land) thrive on logical analysis of business problems, and equally logical solutions. So reasonableness, logic, all that sensible stuff, is wholly good.

But is it?

If we reconsider some of the charismatic and exceptional people we looked at in the last chapter, do we see reasonableness and a love of logic as common characteristics?

It would be difficult to see much that was reasonable about Che Guevara and Fidel Castro deciding to take on the might of the USA with only a handful of friends.

The works of Dalí and Warhol inspire every emotion from outrage to delight; but reasonable and logical are not adjectives many would apply to 'The Great Masturbator' or silkscreen images of an electric chair.

You don't need to concentrate only on those with great charisma: examine the work and the character of any truly successful person, and you don't see logic in the driving seat. More likely you'll see something much more emotional and red-blooded. When Gustave Eiffel built his tower – which has little or no logical purpose – I suspect that reasonableness was the last thing on his mind. He was driven by a passion to produce something startling, something extraordinary, something unique. Was Bill Gates motivated by a reasonable desire to provide improved electronics technology to a wide audience; or by a fierce competitive passion to change people's lives and build a huge commercial empire?

Ask yourself this: if you wanted a simple job done, would you give it to a logical person or a highly passionate person? Me, I'd go for the logical person; and I suspect you would too.

But what if you wanted a really difficult, near-to-impossible job done? At that point, I'd go for the highly passionate person. They might have the raw emotional drive to make the impossible become the possible. Mr Logical would simply explain why it couldn't be done.

There's the rub. Logical, reasonable people are good at ordinary and predictable tasks; the kind of tasks which keep the status quo moving along slowly and sensibly. But give them something which calls for the exceptional, which seeks to change things, which presents a giant challenge, and they just can't hack it. That's when passion matters.

If you want to complete a tax return or repair a dishwasher, go for logic every time. But if you want to overthrow a tyrant or write a sonnet, to solve a great problem or to get people to think in an entirely new way, then go for passion.

This is surprisingly little understood in the business world. Because large businesses appear to offer a high degree of security, they attract employees who are unusually risk-averse. Because the fundamental role of a business is to make more money tomorrow than it made yesterday, there is an overwhelming emphasis on counting in business culture: counting sales, counting costs, counting profits. And a culture which gets preoccupied with the importance of counting soon loses sight of the importance of ideas.

So big business inevitably tends to be staffed by people who are frightened of risk, in a culture where the real power of ideas is neglected in favour of the apparent power of numbers. No wonder they give too much value to logic and not enough to passion.

That's what you should do too, if you merely want to survive in that world.

But if you want to succeed, rather than just survive, you need to think differently.

You need to embrace the energy which passion brings. You need to accept that most big achievements are driven by greed, by ambition, by a mad will to win. Not by a reasonable analysis of all available statistics.

How do you put this into practice in your own working life? Of course, you don't ignore logic and reasonable evaluation: the most passionate person still needs a platform of understanding to work from. But once you have that understanding, then you need to make something happen, to find an answer that wasn't there before.

That's when you shouldn't be frightened of a bit of raw emotion. Trust your instincts about people more and their qualifications less. Back your own judgement and sack the committee. See a mistake as a part of learning, not as a failure. Look before you leap, but don't spend so much time looking that you forget to leap. Don't aim to get things done and not offend someone somewhere. You can't do both. So get on with things; expect some criticism and ignore it when it comes. Put your trust in the quality of ideas rather than the quantity of numbers.

Oh yes, and fire any management consultants you might be using.

In short, put some real emotion into your business life. Trust your heart as well as your head. And be much braver.

Does this need to be more passionate about business life flow into our lives outside business? In many ways, it does. It's sadly true that there is too much prose and not enough poetry in all our lives.

Yet life in business is not the same as life outside. The business world is dominated by large companies, and they are shaped by organization. But our private lives are fundamentally dominated by the family unit, and that is not shaped by organization, but by love and desire. It is desire which brings a couple together; desire which inspires us to have children. And when we do, that desire transmutes to love; for parents' love for their children is surely the most intense emotion we can know. So our family lives, which are at the centre of our social world, are never short of raw emotion in the first place.

What they are short of, though, is a bit of business organization. Family life is, by its very nature, so emotional that it's often hard to deal with things in a calm way.

So let's go back to the basic disciplines of a good pitch and see if that helps:

- Find a calm space to think in.
- Remember that people's emotions count for more than logic.
- Think through your proposition before you spell it out.

- Articulate it in the simplest way.
- Don't go for an unattainable perfect solution, go for what works.
- Focus on what it means to them, not on what it means to you.

Emotion will always be the fundamental force of all that's important in our lives outside work. But applying some business common sense to how we handle those emotions will help you take control of your personal life.

The path to success is clear: be more businesslike about your emotional life, and be more emotional about your business life.

29 Passion beats logic: one simple example

Here's a simple, true story of the power of passion in business. It's a small story, but it makes a big point.

I BEGAN MY business career in advertising, and from the first day it was always my dream to start my own advertising agency.

Eventually, my dream became reality; I started my own business. Our philosophy was straightforward, but ambitious: we wanted to work only with large companies. Small companies had small budgets, and we would avoid them.

After a few years we had a successful business, working with such large international companies as Minolta, Honda and Burberry. Imagine my frustration when one of my partners told me he had agreed that we should pitch for the Mauritius Tourist Office's advertising – a beautiful island, no doubt, but exactly the kind of small budget advertiser I wanted to have nothing to do with.

I argued ferociously, but my colleagues all wanted to go for it – they agreed that it would be small in money, but they also believed it would be big in opportunity. A sexy product like Mauritius would give us the chance to produce sexy advertising that would help make our agency famous. Grudgingly I climbed down; we set to work; and four weeks later the pitch date was upon us. The Mauritian team were due in our office at 2 p.m. that afternoon. I thought of the pitch much as a trip to the dentist: a painful necessity, but in an hour it would be over.

Except that an hour came and went, and no Mauritians arrived. We rang to ask where they were. 'Sorry,' they replied. 'We're running late. Come over to our offices and show us your pitch here.'

Every ad agency prefers to pitch in their own offices, just as a football team prefers to play a home game. To move the venue from our place to theirs was frustrating; to do so when they were already more than an hour late was something between incompetent and plain rude. I was angry.

We also had an important campaign to prepare for Honda cars, our largest client. I'd much rather have been working on that, which made me a lot more angry.

Even so, we packed up all our kit, took a taxi to their office and started to set up our equipment there. When they saw how much we had brought they realized this was going to be a full and serious presentation; and they didn't like that. The head of the Mauritian Tourist Office was a man named Cyril Vadamootoo. Larger than life in several senses, Cyril was a character from a Graham Greene novel – he wore a perfect white linen suit (complete with gold watch-chain across the waistcoat) and needed to lose at least three stone.

Cyril spoke up: 'Look, it's a hot day, we're tired and we've seen seven presentations already. Don't waste our time with all those slides and strategy stuff. Just show us the adverts and we can be through in ten minutes.'

I never wanted to pitch for the business anyway; I was in a

bad mood because they were late and they changed the venue; and now this man was telling us we had ten minutes to show four weeks' work.

I snapped.

I don't know if you are the same, but if I lose my temper in a small way I tend to be noisy and shout a bit; but if I lose my temper in a big way I'm icily calm.

I started (calmly) to pack up our kit again and put it back in its cases, and I gave Cyril my card. 'You clearly don't have time to see our presentation today,' I said. 'So here's my number. When you're next in London, with time to spare, give me a call and we'd be happy to show it to you.'

I started to walk out with my disgruntled team (I'll never know whether they were disgruntled with me or with him) following reluctantly.

'Hold on, we can give you a bit more than ten minutes: half an hour would be fine,' they said.

'Fine for you, but not for me,' I replied. 'We've worked on this – free – for a month, and we show it on our terms or not at all.'

'OK, we can give you an hour . . .'

'You're not listening; I'm not going to negotiate how long it takes to give you our advice. Goodbye.'

We left their offices and started to look for a taxi, when one of the Mauritian team appeared and breathlessly told us we could have as long as we wanted.

We went back, and we gave our pitch.

The next morning, Cyril Vadamootoo arrived, unannounced, at my office. Another immaculate linen suit, this time in pale beige, but still with the gold watch-chain across the waistcoat.

'I came to tell you that you've won the business,' he said. 'It wasn't because of your presentation; it was because you stood up to us and you wouldn't be bullied. We're a small country and we can behave small-time on occasions. We need partners who will be strong with us.'

My loss of temper had been a triumph of passion over logic, but it had won us the business.

We went on to do famous advertising for Mauritius, which was widely noticed and talked about, in spite of their modest budget. It won a bundle of awards for us, and helped us dramatically in building our business. It also won a huge amount of holiday business for Mauritius; and since tourism is their main industry, it had a significant effect on the island's economy.

So, my outburst of temper secured us a contract which not only transformed our company but also transformed the economy of a small and very beautiful country.

Just one example of how powerful passion can be.

30 When pitching changed the world

In 2016, the world's geo-political landscape suffered not one but two major earthquakes. Both were utterly unexpected.

First, DAVID Cameron (recently re-elected as Prime Minister with an increased majority) called a referendum to endorse Britain's continued membership of the European Union. Against all the polls and all the expectations, he lost. Britain was on its way out of Europe: and Cameron was on his way out of office.

Second, and even more startlingly, a property magnate-cum-reality show TV host decided to run for the Presidency of the USA. With neither political experience nor credibility, he offered a barrage of quasi-hysterical opinions, and little else. No-one took him seriously as a candidate. A few turbulent months later he was inaugurated as the 45th President of the United States.

The first of these two upheavals, Cameron's downfall, is largely due to how he pitched his case. Or, to be more exact, how he failed to pitch it.

And the second upheaval, Trump's triumph, is also largely due to how he pitched his case.

To say 'Life's a Pitch' is no exaggeration, when we see that world affairs can turn on one man's ability to present his case. Didn't we start this book by saying that pitching is important, because it changes things?

Let's examine these two episodes to see what we can learn from them. After all, one is a perfect example of 'how to', while the other is a perfect example of 'how not to'.

Cameron: a career collapses in one night

What makes Cameron's failure particularly surprising is the fact that his rise to power was rooted in his gift as a communicator. The story of how he won his first candidacy as a Member of Parliament appears earlier in this book; and his experience before politics was in Public Relations. Yet when it came to Europe, the issue he had made the test of his leadership, he stumbled and fell. What went wrong?

At the heart of many Brexiteers' resistance to the European project was a strong fear of immigration. There was a belief that our island, and our precious resources, were being overrun by immigrants, mostly from Eastern Europe. Cameron side-stepped the immigration issue, perhaps because he knew how emotionally charged it would be. But by side-stepping this issue, he was implicitly accepting the arguments of his opponents.

And there is a counter-argument. Imagine, for example, the National Health Service without foreign workers, be they a humble cleaner or an experienced physician. Anyone who has been in an NHS hospital for more than about two minutes can see that without immigrant labour there just wouldn't be enough people to go round: the NHS would grind to a halt. But Cameron didn't talk about it.

Similarly, there was a groundswell of British opinion which thought that the sovereignty of our parliament was being usurped by a gang of overpaid bureaucrats in Brussels. In truth, that's largely nonsense: decisions on our education system, our health system, our policing, and our national budget are all made in the UK by the UK parliament. The focus of the Brussels bureaucrats is on trade, where we have a vested interest in playing by the same rules as our trading partners as the price for sharing the same market. Again, Cameron didn't talk about this.

Whereas Cameron was suicidally understated, his opponents were vociferous. They even had a 'battle bus' which toured the country displaying a huge claim that after Brexit we could stop paying the EU £350 million a week, and spend it on the NHS instead.

This claim was a flagrant lie. Technically, we do pay £350 million a week into EU coffers, but in practice we have a rebate, negotiated by Margaret Thatcher in the 1980s. It's a complex formula, but the UK Treasury estimates it at around half of our total payment. Added to which, while it's true that we pay in to the EU, it's also true that the EU pays into us. We receive, for example, big subsidies for farmers, and big contributions to our universities. So the Brexiteers' claim was a lie; and demonstrably so. But Cameron didn't demon-strate it. By ignoring the lie, by letting it go unchallenged and unexposed, he allowed it to grow into a half-truth.

An important point emerges from this: if you are pitching against strongly held opinions, you can't ignore them. Not recognizing a concern doesn't make it go away: it encourages it to fester.

In a case like this, you have to refute the more disingenuous claims of the other side. But you also have to make some claims of your own. You have to stand for something. Cameron singularly failed to spell out in a vivid and simple way what the advantage of EU membership was. He seemed to imply that as long as we stayed in the EU, everything would carry on happily as it had before. But plenty of voters didn't think that 'carrying on' was enough. They were living in a world where the politicians had too much of the power and the people had too little of the money. They didn't want to preserve the *status quo*, they wanted to change it.

The audience of any pitch wants to believe that the future is going to be better than the past. If you're the marketing head of BMW listening to an ad agency pitching for your business, you want to hear how BMW sales are going to go up. If you're a young woman listening to a marriage proposal, you hope that marriage will bring you joys you hadn't had before. In the eighteenth century, Dr Johnson asserted that –

'Promise, large promise, is the soul of an advertisement.'

How little has changed in 250 years. Unsurprisingly, Dr Johnson put it better and simpler than I can. But the message is the same: folk want things to get better, and if you don't tell them that'll happen, they'll assume that it won't. And then they'll vote for the other guy.

So Cameron was guilty of failing to grasp the nettle: he didn't engage strongly in the debate. He failed to refute his opponents' claims, even when they were patently dishonest. Above all, he failed to advance his own case with 'promise, large promise'.

But beyond the level of debate, of claim and counter-claim, Cameron made the one mistake no pitcher should ever make: he behaved as if he'd won already. His body language was that of a man dealing with a foregone conclusion. Only an idiot would vote to leave, he seemed to imply.

Most people don't care to be thought of as an idiot, nor do they wish to be patronized. While a good pitcher should never be sycophantic (crawling is a sign of weakness), he should not be complacent either. The tone to strike is one of enthusiasm, underpinned by a modest degree of confidence.

You wouldn't vote for an unconfident leader. But you wouldn't vote for a complacent one either. Cameron took his audience for granted, and on the night of 23rd June 2016, 52% of them took their revenge. By lunchtime the next day, he was out of a job.

I said earlier in this book that every good presentation has, at its heart, a strong, simple idea. Cameron's campaign lacked that strong, simple idea.

I wonder, in his enforced early retirement, if he ever reflects on how he made his pitch?

Being Prime Minister is a tough job. But for Cameron, not being Prime Minister may prove to be tougher.

Truth stranger than fiction: the inexorable rise of Donald Trump

How often do you hear people say about a real, though surprising, event: 'You couldn't make it up'?

It seems to be a growing refrain.

Indeed, if you read J.G. Ballard's novel, *Crash*, he has written a brilliant introduction which explores, with philosophical eloquence, how truth and fiction seem to be increasingly transposed in the world we inhabit today:

> 'I feel that the balance between fiction and reality has changed significantly in the past decades. Increasingly, their roles are reversed. We live in a world ruled by fictions of every kind – mass merchandising, advertising, politics conducted as a branch of advertising, the pre-empting of any original response to experience by the television screen. We live inside an enormous novel. It is now less and less necessary for the writer to invent the fictional content of his novel. The fiction is already there.'

Ballard wrote this in 1973; and his pessimism is clear to see. But even he could never have imagined that a generation later, the most powerful man in the world would ascend to that height, not through public service or a life in politics, but after a career as a property dealer and the host of a TV show.

How did that astonishing event occur?

The answer to this huge question is, in fact, remarkably uncomplicated. Trump, outsider though he was, pitched his case with strength and simplicity – while his rival, Hillary Clinton, singularly failed to do that.

If we're going to learn anything useful from Trump's astonishing victory, it's important to distinguish between his politics, which I find abhorrent, and his pitching skills, which won him the presidency against all odds.

There are two recurring themes in this book: first, a successful pitch starts with an understanding of the needs of your audience; and second, you must meet those needs with a strong, simple idea.

Now apply those themes to the 2016 election battle. Trump realized that there was a swathe of middle America whose prosperity was waning fast and whose patience with the political class was waning even faster. He targeted that group with ruthless persistence. He never fell into the trap of trying to be all things to all people: indeed, he seemed to relish attacking Mexicans, Muslims, the political elite, the media, and just about everyone else – except that hard core of disillusioned middle America.

He offered that group a clear and confident promise: 'We'll make America great again'. He spoke directly to all those who felt disenfranchised, emotionally and financially, and he gave them *hope*.

There was, for me, a decisive moment in one of the early TV debates between Trump and Hillary Clinton. Trump was banging on, as usual, about 'Make America great again' and Hillary intervened with what she clearly thought was a match-winning insight.

'Actually, Donald,' she said, 'America is already great'.

It may well have been a match-winning comment. Trouble was, it won the fight for Trump not Hillary. Because, if you deconstruct what she said, it really meant 'I'm OK with how things are now'. And that in turn means, 'Vote for me and nothing will change'.

We're back to Dr Johnson and 'Promise, large promise, is the soul of an advertisement'. Trump's promise was a return to greatness. Hillary was only promising the *status quo*.

She may well have been right: America was already great. But that wasn't the message voters wanted to hear. They wanted the hope of a better future.

And they voted for the candidate who offered that.

To the intelligentsia, Trump represented something quite hideous: a vain vulgarian who could barely string an articulate sentence together. Hardly White House material. But to Trump's target audience, the disaffected of America's traditional industrial heartland, he was a man who recognized their problem. And showed an obsessive determination to resolve it.

He was clever enough to resist any temptation to tone down his maverick persona. Ever the contrarian, he revelled in it. The result was that the electorate saw Trump as a flesh and blood human being, warts and all, not the sanitized two-dimensional construct of a political PR guru.

Trump was a much smarter electioneer than his critics realized.

Of course, to those who instinctively shied away from him, this only emphasized his unsuitability for office. But to those who were drawn to him, it made his charisma all the more powerful. And he energized enough of these people to win the prize he coveted.

I saw Trump on television at one of his early rallies, when he was still very much an outsider for the Republican candidacy, let alone the presidency. At that time, he was being publicly mocked for his absurdly over-coiffured, and presumably dyed, hairstyle. It was a symbol of too much vanity and too little gravitas. He simply didn't look the part.

Trump tackled this head on. He started his speech with a bizarre question—

'What is the difference between a raccoon and Donald Trump's hairstyle?'

He allowed a brief pause after this very non-presidential question; and then, loudly, he enunciated his own answer—

'A raccoon doesn't have $8 billion!'

It was a masterstroke. English culture worships tradition; Italian culture worships style; German culture worships efficiency. But American culture worships money. In the USA, financial success is what it's all about. And Trump had branded himself as a financial success, writ large. He'd even made this brash boast in a way that showed he was able to laugh at himself – or at least at his haircut.

(Since his election, this talent for self-deprecation seems to have evaporated rather quickly. But when did we expect political candidates to behave after the election the way they did before?)

I've always abhorred Trump's vanity as much as I've abhorred his values. But when I heard the raccoon joke, it was immediately clear that here was a man who knew how to play his audience. He had sensed from the ridicule inspired by his haircut that the criticism went beyond the superficial: he appeared to lack seriousness.

Trump responded brilliantly: he met the criticism directly and with a dash of humour. He turned it into an opportunity to use his wealth as evidence of his gift as a manager. If he can make that fortune for himself, surely he can restore the fortunes of America?

Voters in the rust belt were mesmerized. Here was the man who could give back the hope they thought they'd lost forever. And whereas other politicians all seemed to be cardboard cut-outs, determined to offend no-one, here was a real human being: flawed and passionate, but real.

For example, his response to being accused of groping women was not to deny the behaviour, but to treat it almost as a perk of office. Hillary supporters expected female voters to desert him in droves. But in the event, it almost seemed to enhance his charisma: many women saw it as evidence of a man behaving like men often do – and at least he wasn't lying about it. Trump was, for better or for worse, a real man with real passions. This was in sharp contrast with Hillary, who came across as too prepared, too polished, too perfect to exhibit much human warmth.

Whether Trump stands the test of time as a great president remains to be seen. Personally, I have doubts. But his skill as a pitcher can't be challenged. He won the Republican candidacy from the position of a complete outsider, and he went on to win the presidency from an equally parlous place.

What can we learn from his success?

First, he understood his audience. He knew that middle America had lost heart; and felt, literally, impoverished. He focused his promise on that group, and resolutely refused to compromise it to widen his appeal.

Second, he had a strong, simple message. He would 'Make America great again'. He repeated that message with a splendid disdain for subtlety. It was on baseball caps, it was on banners, it peppered every speech. The policies behind the promise may not have convinced all of us – will that wall ever be built? But the promise itself was clear and confident. And it rang out often.

Lastly, he burnished his own charisma. Most of us hold back from showing our feelings to the fullest. We're worried about what others may think. Trump had no such anxiety. He behaved with an outrageous self-belief and an equally outrageous disregard for convention. The result was someone who stood out from the ordinary. This may have inspired distaste in many. But it inspired admiration in enough to win him the most powerful post in the world.

For Donald Trump, as for the rest of us, life truly is a pitch.

Book
2

1 First impressions:
on being well presented, or, Yo, Blair!

W<small>E GIVE</small> a first impression whether we want to or not, so best to make it work for you. Every time we meet someone, we scroll through conscious and unconscious responses to what we see or what we hear (or even smell or feel: just think of that slippery handshake). Then we form judgements about who's in charge, and those judgements determine the destiny of the relationship. Did you ever hear anybody say, 'He makes a really wonderful third impression!'?

The most famous Presidential–Prime Ministerial exchange ever was an example of this. Of course, they had met before (and lasting first impressions had clearly been made), but Bush II's 'Yo, Blair!' was an appellation of genius. At once establishing an element of intimacy which helpfully excluded those present at the summit who were not beneficiaries of our delusional Special Relationship, Bush's patronizing adoption of the demotic and insolent use of the surname immediately established an easy superiority. As I recall from the video, the President did not even bother to rise from his seat to deliver this devastating put-down, thus further enhancing his status as Commander-in-Chief.

Prime Ministers get about a lot, so these are risks they have to take. But it's fine if you prefer to stay at home alone. Some people do. In fact, the mathematician and thinker Blaise Pascal said the general inability to be solitary was the source of much of the world's unhappiness. Anti-social in later life, Pascal came to believe: 'Plus je vois l'homme, plus j'aime mon chien.' (The more I see of man, the more I love my dog.) Yet, cursed with sociability, we insist on moving about and around. It may make us unhappy, all this movement, but there are no clear signs that people are returning to Pascal's idiosyncratic version of solitary confinement.

Indeed, staying at home alone can be productive of anxiety, as Franz Kafka knew. 'There is no need for you to leave the house,' he wrote. 'Stay at your table and listen. Don't even listen, just wait. Don't even wait, be completely quiet and alone. The world will offer itself to you to be unmasked.' Well, maybe, but this connoisseur of anxiety was happier on internal journeys than external ones. Amazingly. Kafka's *Amerika* (1927), a vivid fiction, was written without actually visiting the United States.

But, Pascal and Kafka notwithstanding, there's a reasonable argument that going out and about into the world is a defining condition of humanity, if not quite as busily as Tony Blair once did. The psychologist Alfred Adler said that moving around stimulated the mind because it entailed risk and required effective stratagems for security and survival. What good would it do a plant to have a mind, he argued, since with no power of movement the plant could not act on any thought that might occur to it. Physical movement has actually contributed to intellectual evolution, as Shakespeare noted: 'Sense, sure, you have,/Else you could not have motion', according to Hamlet.

For humans, movement abroad usually entails social activity. And as soon as you socialize, you are acting. Step out of the house, walk the street or enter a room and the rules change.

When you are not alone, you are being watched and analysed. You are performing as if in a play. Shakespeare again – indeed, the whole of literature – is full of metaphorical references to the world being a theatre, a place where we have to take our cues. Of course, Shakespeare's own theatre acknowledged this interplay between the artificial stage and the real world in its name: the Globe. King Lear says, 'When we are born, we cry that we are come/To this great stage of fools.' The question here is how best to act with the fools, how to prepare your script and how to act on the stage of fools.

Well, no need to be that upset about it. Better to direct this stage of fools into a well-rehearsed performance, preferably one of your own invention. Once out of solitary confinement and beyond subsistence existence, you are acting and your performance will be judged by the people you meet. There are no options or evasions in this contract: value-free neutrality does not exist. Even the person who says, 'I don't care what people think about my appearance,' actually declares the opposite. He is merely confirming an acute awareness of what people think, that he is exquisitely sensitive to how he is perceived and received. He merely wishes to make the point that he is not prepared to follow conventional expectations in matters of style and manners. It is just another way of confirming that appearances matter.

Privacy : The secret formula of self

The first impression you make may be a public phenomenon, but it was developed in the privacy of your own imagination.

Privacy is not about pulling down the shutters and

wrapping our head in dense Welsh horse blanket, but about personal identity, sex, hygiene, human rights, architectural space, religious contemplation and creative solitude. Now the internet, social media, metadata, hacking and CCTV surveillance all threaten it. Privacy is extremely precious, but it is under threat and needs to be saved.

Our contemporary notion of privacy is an invention of recent history, not much older than the steam engine. Its creation was intimately involved with the evolving modern idea of 'personality', the belief that each of us has distinctive traits, that our 'self' has a secret formula.

But privacy is not the same as mere secrecy. Privacy includes ideas about personal freedom and the organization of culture.

Privacy did not exist in the historic past and does not exist in all cultures. When the traveller Sir Richard Burton found Arab women bathing naked in an oasis, they spontaneously covered their faces when they realized they were being spied-on by European men. Their religion taught them that the face was more a 'private part' than the sexual organs. Meanwhile, in the European Middle Ages, eating, bathing and sleeping were communal. It was only in the nineteenth century that a woman might bathe without attendants.

Western notions of cultivated life have many different versions of privacy: the monk in his cell, the artist in his atelier, the *hortus conclusus*, Thoreau in his hut on Walden Pond. Proust is full of references to the creative benefits of solitude (a theme persuasively developed by psychiatrist Anthony Storr). Indeed, a recurrent motif in Victorian literature is the secret room. As Patrick Leigh-Fermor explained in *A Time to Keep Silence*, the monastic retreat is the best remedy for urban anxiety. In domestic architecture, we value the interplay between shared space and personal space. Few would want to live in a house with no privacy.

The UN Declaration of Human Rights includes privacy, a forensic idea that can be traced back to *The Harvard Law Review* of 1890 in an article by Samuel D. Warren and Louis Brandeis called 'The Right to Privacy'. When our privacy is threatened, so too is our freedom and even the integrity of our personality, yet so many of the pressures in contemporary life conspire to reduce the individual's access to privacy. A person who cultivates privacy sets himself apart from the controlling forces of contemporary life. Thus, advocating privacy is a privilege that is contrary to an accepted order which, for the moment at least, values instant access to information, experiences and merchandise above serious and pleasurable contemplation of them.

Ideas about privacy are culturally determined. There is no exact Italian equivalent and Russian uses a word semantically half way between 'secrecy' and 'private life'. Our contemporary notion of 'privacy' is essentially Anglo-American, an expression of our concerns and preoccupations and our culture's institutionalized megalomania. Private Dining, Private Medicine and Private Banking are ways of defining our unique personalities.

Despite the invasions of CCTV and data-mining, that we value privacy so highly is indicated by the fact that medical records and voting histories are fiercely protected by law and most of us would prefer our intimate activities to be our own, not the public's. And intrusions into privacy are often illegal. But there are contrary forces: crowd-sourcing is now promoted above creative solitude – although a crowd-sourced song is yet to be a hit. Still, the internet wants to find out everything about you. And, unless you burn your smartphone, it can. Maybe 'privacy' was only a passing moment, just like the steam engine. Maybe in future everything will be explicit and shared, instantaneous and cheap, here today and gone tomorrow. Then again, in a better future, maybe not.

An interesting complication in the inevitable task of acting a role as ourselves in the outside world is that we are all more than one personality. Which one to choose? Oliver Goldsmith caught the delicious paradox beautifully when he described the character of the actor David Garrick: 'On the stage he was natural, simple, affecting; 'twas only that when he was off he was acting.' Garrick was always two people: the professional actor who was always convincing and the off-duty human being . . . who was also performing, but often less impressively. Poets are often painfully aware of matters of identity. With deliberate illiteracy, Rimbaud wrote: 'Je est un autre.' ('I is another.')

No one ever cared more about appearances than Marcel Proust. When told at unnecessary length of the diplomatic intricacies of the Treaty of Versailles, Proust

When we are born, we cry that we are come/To this great stage of fools

winced and said he was only really interested in the colour of the blotting paper the eminent signatories used. Always keen on the uneasy relationship between seeing and believing, Proust thought there might be a second chance in the matter of making first impressions. Since he believed that every personality is destroyed as soon as people cease to observe it, he convinced himself that for any individual his next appearance – his reappearance – presented an opportunity for a personal redesign. Well, maybe. Whether first, second or third impressions, there is no more arresting task than working on this project. Vanity and megalomania may be unattractive, but effective self-expression is perhaps the dominant necessity of cultivated human nature.

So, let's assess the material we are working with. What is a human being? The scientific answer: 96.2 per cent of you is organic elements, including the proteins of RNA and DNA, lipids and sugars. And then there's oxygen, carbon, hydrogen and nitrogen, water and carbon dioxide. Plus 1.5 per cent calcium and 0.3 per cent sulphur. Oh yes, traces of chromium, molybdenum, vanadium, tin and zinc. But chemistry rather ignores the poetry. Generally, most of us are three distinct personalities:

1. **The person we think we are**
2. **The person others think we are**
3. **The person we believe others think we are**

Maybe the great task in modern life is to reconcile this disparate trinity into a fully functioning whole, with seamless distinctions, so that conflicts between self-awareness and other people's judgements no longer exist. Maybe this is impossible, but if life's a pitch, why not make it a successful one?

The search for an authentic expression of self is not straightforward. The great sociologist Erving Goffman, in his landmark study *The Presentation of Self in Everyday Life* (1959), asked the deceptively simple question: is there any such thing as a 'real' personality? He doubted it. It may give encouragement to career charlatans to learn that academic sociologists have some doubts about the verifiable nature of reality, but it is true that no sentient being ever responds unselfconsciously to the crude facts of any situation. Apart from shivering in an arctic wind or purring in summer sunshine, our behaviour is not a simple matter of input and response: that's the way cabbages behave. Our autonomic nervous system is always influenced by social, cultural, financial and sexual interests. Consideration of these interests is the 'front' we design for ourselves. Only race and size are difficult to change, but advances in surgery and cosmetics mean even these aspects of ourselves are no longer as fixed as they were at the Creation. To a degree, you have inevitably designed yourself. You have responded to the situational proprieties. And this is why first impressions matter.

But this is not to say that the desolate Existentialist Jean-Paul Sartre was right when he wrote in Nausea (1938) that 'Things are entirely what they appear to be – and behind them ... there is nothing.' Disgust and self-hatred were Sartre's disagreeable themes, but you do not need to be a gloomy existentialist to appreciate that surfaces are extremely important. True, only shallow people do not judge by appearances, but appearances are not self-dependent. On the contrary, things are very rarely exactly as they seem.

A surprising degree of dissimulation, or at least calculation, is often involved from the start of any human exchange. People ask, 'How are you?' Actually, few really care. In fact, the fabric of civilized exchange would begin to disintegrate if this sticky question were ever dealt with honestly. 'Actually, I have an embarrassing rash, my daughter's on the game, and I am ashamed of my car,' is a rare response to this most familiar enquiry. As banker J. Pierpont Morgan said, there are two reasons for doing or saying something. One that sounds good . . . and then the real one.

And the language of first impressions is by no means always verbal. Nancy Mitford has a character in *Love in a Cold Climate* (1949) who trains herself to say 'brush' on entering a room because the labial contortions necessary to enunciate the word tend to fix a pleasing smile on the face; thus she arms herself for the pitch while disarming the audience.

> **First impressions are generally based on a spontaneous assessment of:**
> 1. Status
> 2. Clothes
> 3. Sex
> 4. Age
> 5. Size and posture
> 6. Speech
> 7. Facial expressions and non-verbal communications

These will all be dealt with later in the book, but let's gloss them here.

Status

The traditional feudal apparatus of status, of, say, gilt carriages and liveried footmen, has transferred directly to the modern world. Stratagems of arrival remain influential: making an entrance has a metaphorical significance beyond the stage. A design consultant once said you have to arrive in a BMW, otherwise the client won't take you seriously. Few influential bankers use buses, or what Americans call 'loser cruisers'. On the other hand, walking to appointments often impresses. In business, the briefcase has acquired inverted status. Once a symbol of 'executive' authority, possession of one now more likely indicates the opposite. The man who comes to fix the dishwasher carries his tools in a briefcase. Off the street and into a room, a certain gravitas is achieved by dignity in motion. The self-assured rarely fidget and often move with solemnity.

Clothes

When the lobbies of great hotels are populated by people in shorts and bumbags, conventional notions of how to be well presented may be misleading, but underlying principles remain. There are many arguments in favour of what the poet Robert Herrick called 'delight in disorder', but there are none in favour of being a careless, malodorous, unsightly slob. In one of his many *Letters to His Son* (this written in 1753), Lord Chesterfield says, 'Dress is a very foolish thing; and yet it is a very foolish thing for a man not to be well dressed.' It is more a matter of detail and finish than of style and fashion: in *The Valet as Historian*, a witty guide to terrible acts of betrayal by wardrobes, Beverley Nichols said, 'I have met my share of the great of the earth and usually have found that their

> **Dress is a very foolish thing; and yet it is a very foolish thing for a man not to be well dressed**

trousers have been as eloquent as their lips.' In Manhattan many years later, Jay McInerney says much the same thing about footwear: 'You won't be judged by your accent . . . but you will be judged by your shoes.' The old adage that it should take ten minutes before you realize a gentleman is well dressed may not survive into a world of high-tops and hoodies, but remains a useful stimulus towards elegant understatement.

Sex

Awareness of gender is fundamental and, except in very specialized circumstances, rarely ambiguous. Mark Knapp, an American researcher, found, in an imaginative experiment, that adding two inches to the padding of a bra increased a female hitchhiker's success rate in getting lifts. There are no decorous equivalents offering a similar advantage to men, although the fact of sexual awareness, let alone evidence of curiosity or promise of availability, remains significant in forming first impressions.

Age

A perception of seniority, or its opposite, is a fundamental element in forming a first impression of anyone.

Size and posture

The novelist Joseph Heller has eloquently explained that famous people are always perceived as being tall and, concomitantly, the public is often confused when their favourite political or sports or entertainment celebrity turns out, as is so often the case, to be surprisingly short. Pilates teachers believe that for impressive posture, pelvic floor exercises are necessary, a useful discipline when faced with a demanding introduction or a camera. This involves willing the ascent of the rectum without compressing the cheeks of the bottom.

Speech

The manner of speaking is decisive in forming first impressions. As in professional broadcasting, a sense of relaxation is hard won and spontaneity has usually to be calculated. Content is just as important. Say little, but say it well and say it short: the art of boring someone is to tell them everything. Again, favourable first impressions are made by courtesy. A gentleman, it used to be said, is someone who is never rude . . . unintentionally.

> **A gentleman, it used to be said, is someone who is never rude . . . unintentionally.**

Facial expressions and non-verbal communications

Chesterfield again: 'Frequent and loud laughter is the characteristic of folly and ill manners.' 'Put soul into every handclap' was Elbert Hubbard's advice. Italians have developed a language of gestures so refined and so expressive that designer Bruno Munari has published a *Supplemento al Dizionario Italiano* (1963) with photographs and explanations of how a conversation may be prosecuted by hand alone.

> **Put soul into every handclap**

These aspects of first impressions – what Erving Goffmann called 'patterned adaptations to the rules' – are the fundamentals of how we see others, and the fundamentals too of how people see us and should be considered as we work on the project of designing ourselves. In considering status, posture, conversation, hand gestures and facial expressions, we can improve on Nature with a process of Unnatural Selection. Evolutionary biologist Richard Dawkins says Nature is intelligent, although to the rest of us it looks more like a lottery where the thoughtful person will feel the need to influence the numbers. The brief to design yourself leads to fascinating questions about self-identity.

William James, the novelist's brother and a pioneer of psychical research, was a pioneer in thinking of how personalities were created. In *The Varieties of Religious Experience* (1902) he was keen to emphasize how little the orthodox anti-material philosophy could contribute to a real understanding of man's predicament in the modern world. With a fine disregard for distinctions between 'me' and 'mine', James explained that 'A man's self is the sum total of all that he can call his, not only his body and his psychic powers, but his clothes and his house, his wife and children, his ancestors and friends, his reputation and works, his lands and houses and yacht and bank account.' James was a founder of the Pragmatists, a philosophical school that interprets the meaning of things in terms of their practical effects. To James, a belief or an idea was true and good if it made you happier, irrespective – almost – of its relationship to scientifically verifiable accuracy. He also had a very handy equation for measuring personal achievement:

$$\text{Success} = \frac{\text{Status}}{\text{Pretensions}}$$

In other words, it is not merely what we think that makes us what we are, but how we look and what we possess, whether our BMW, our trousers or our shoes, are also features that determine our personalities. George Santayana, an associate of James, described this complex edifice in an essay on 'The Socialized Self' published in *Soliloquies* (1922): 'Our animal habits are transmuted by conscience into loyalties and duties, and we become "personae" or masks.' Significantly, the etymology of the word 'person' goes back to 'mask', suggesting that a need to disguise and dissimulate the 'real' self, to provide first impressions which are designed rather than natural, is pre-Homeric. To the ancients, the spirit resided in the face, so to disguise the face was a defensive necessity.

The most effective self-designers actually believe their performance. Novelist Kurt Vonnegut said we are what we pretend to be and those who pretend with the most efficacy are what we tend to call sincere, although people who are not actually taken in by the impression they – or others – have decided to make are what we disparage as 'cynical'! So deep is the need for effective disguise through the successful management of first impressions, those who see through it threaten the established order. Brett Easton Ellis has a character who says, disturbingly, 'You do a very good impression of yourself.'

Frequent articles in *The American Journal of Psychiatry* tell alarming stories about mental patients who exaggerate their condition – who act 'mad' – so as not to disappoint the expectations of student doctors. Hollywood and the media are (one is tempted to write 'naturally') fertile ground to explore for perverse examples of self-design, although Sanskrit, courtly romances of the European Middle Ages and Wagner all also contain stories about people who, in pretending to be other people pretending to be them, are in fact masquerading as themselves. It is so widespread, the assumption must be that the need for dissimulation and disguise is a human universal.

At the very least, it is clear that one of the most difficult of tasks is to get an accurate impression of how exactly others see us. In his masterpiece of self-help, *How To Win Friends and Influence People* (1936), Dale Carnegie quotes a disappointed Al Capone. The murderous mobster was most displeased with the impression he formed in others: 'I have spent the best years of my life giving people the lighter pleasures, helping them have a good time, and all I get is abuse,' he complained. A more palatable American character had a more elegiac take on impressions. Gerald Murphy, the rich socialite and artist, a French Riviera and Long Island legend, who said 'living well is the best revenge', was the model

I have spent the best years of my life giving people the lighter pleasures, helping them have a good time, and all I get is abuse

for Dick Diver in *Tender is the Night*. After the death of his two children he told Scott Fitzgerald, 'Only the invented parts of our life had any meaning.'

There are some marvellous stories about the pleasures and perils of self-design in Wendy Doniger's *The Woman Who Pretended to Be Who She Was* (2005). First there was Cary Grant, a humble lad from Bristol who was translated through the mechanism of the movies into a superbly dressed, laid-back

American sophisticate in handmade silk suits and cashmere cardigans. Grant, real name Archibald Alexander Leach, said with a mixture of humour and despair, 'Everyone wants to be Cary Grant. Even I want to be Cary Grant.' Other splendid invented names include Elton John for Reginald Kenneth Dwight and Whoopi Goldberg for Caryn Elaine Johnson.

Then there was Mick Jagger who spent decades practising the art and then cultivating the image of being a diabolically seductive and effective lover. A female groupie, long in pursuit, one night satisfied her curiosity by bedding the lead singer of the Rolling Stones. Reporting back to her enquiring friends she said, 'He was great, but he was no Mick Jagger.' Pressure of public expectation can force strange distortions on even the most carefully wrought examples of self-design.

Thus there is no better – or worse – example of Vonnegut's precept about becoming what we pretend to be than Ernest Hemingway. Critic Dwight Macdonald described Hemingway's *Across the River and into the Trees* (1950) as 'self-parody of almost unbelievable fatuity'. Later critics described Papa's descent into ludicrous self-imitation when the first impression he offered visitors was as a lumberjack/hunter/drunk with a tendency to sentiment who spoke in a mixture of feral grunts, Navajo and sporting metaphors. Even Lillian Ross could not tolerate the pose with its sadism and facetiousness. So who is to say, but perhaps the conflict between the 'real' Hemingway and his utterly convincing self-designed persona, or mask, was, together with the depressive effects of Olympic alcoholism and unsatisfactory marriages, the reason why one Idaho morning in 1961 the matador, hunter, journalist, boxer, freedom-fighter, lover and Nobel Prize winner blew his head off with a hunting rifle.

Anthony Storr had a sound belief, possibly influenced by Alfred Adler's *What Life Should Mean to You* (1933), that the best possible test for psychological health is the ability to get on with

> **The best possible test for psychological health is the ability to get on with other people**

other people. In this sense self-design that fails to make a good impression, as Hemingway found increasingly the case later in life, is doubly damning: you have deceived yourself without delighting others. Still, for the rest of us, effective self-parody may actually be the closest we get to authenticity.

So, if we are not going to stay home alone, admiring Pascal's dog, what are the criteria for making and receiving favourable first impressions? In 1750 Lord Chesterfield told his son that whenever he met anybody useful, 'Feed him, and feed upon him at the same time.' This stratagem was devised to give an impression of being knowledgeable and a helpful impression of admiring knowledge in others. Dale Carnegie said we should be absolutely certain to smile.

Carnegie was not too timid to prioritize what we expect from life. In a fascinating order which richly deserves separate analysis, he wrote:

1. Health 2. Food 3. Sleep 4. Money 5. Afterlife 6. Sex 7. Children 8. Status

This list can perhaps be simplified to that basic law of human interaction, which says there is no point in engaging anyone in conversation unless they satisfy one (or, preferably, all) of three requirements:

1. An ability to make you laugh or reflect
2. A suggestion of possible future – or, indeed, imminent – sexual gratification
3. A suggestion of being able to give you money

If this is an act you can perform or if it is an act you have experienced, if the first impression you give or get combines wit, sex and money, if this is true, then it has been a good pitch. Otherwise, best to stay home alone.

SUMMARY

FIRST IMPRESSIONS

❏ It's an act, so rehearse.

❏ But it's not a rehearsal, it's real.

❏ You are what you pretend to be.

❏ Judge and be judged by appearances.

❏ If it makes you happy, do it.

❏ Make every encounter a work of art.

2 A history of charlatanism and camouflage, or, lessons from impression management

YOU CAN learn from charlatans. There is a rich history of professional deception that can be as practically inspiring as it is morally dismaying. But what can be learnt from professional deceivers?

A pitch is about persuasion, about making a favourable impression in order to win a deal or an argument. Or, indeed, to win approval in matters of friendship, either sexual or social. And while it may sound cynical to say so, most forms of persuasion involve an element of deception. Sometimes self-deception, because in persuading others we often convince ourselves and become that which we pretend to be.

❛ Plato knew there were three elements in human motivation: reason, love and the desire for recognition and approval ❜

The mask we design for these performances might well be what the elegant philosopher-boulevardier George Santayana called 'faithful, discreet and superlative', but it may also be deceitful. Yet that mask is real, substantial and important.

Appearances are paramount here. A pitch may not necessarily be grounded in cold scientific fact or rigid logic or eternal philosophical truth, but then neither are the theatre or music. Great art does not have to be 'true'. History has many lessons for the modern pitchman. Magicians and mountebanks, acrobats, ventriloquists, *saltimbanques* and *bateleurs*, cow-town evangelists, circus promoters, hucksters with snake oil, charlatans with their tricks and hustles, all practised presentational devices which are essentially similar to a pitch.

Plato knew there were three elements in human motivation: reason, love and the desire for recognition and approval. This last he called *thymos*, but more pertinent to modern thinking is the fact that the word prestige (the type of recognition most of us crave) is next to prestidigitation in the dictionary; indeed, they are etymologically linked. The primary definition of prestige is 'a delusion'. A prestidigator is one who practises sleight of hand, who juggles with words as well as his fingers (*digitus* in Latin). He is a charlatan with nimble (*presto* in Latin) fingers and an even more nimble mind. We can learn from him. Charlatans need energy, resource and imagination. They need to be good with words, to have the genius of persuasion. Other rogues and ne'er-do-wells – rapists, murderers, conmen, poisoners, fraudsters, assassins, swindlers – are more one-dimensional. Charlatans need scope and use imagination. A point arrives where charlatanism becomes art.

The word charlatan comes from the Italian *ciarlare*, which means to prate or babble; a charlatan pretends to knowledge or expertise, is a master of deception and persuasion and impressions. There have been many colourful examples in history. Theophrastus Philippus Aureolus Bombastus von

Hohenheim, an itinerant early sixteenth-century medic, was among the first. He assumed the name Paracelsus on the basis that he was, at least in his own estimation, superior to Celsus, the celebrated first century AD physician. His overbearing personality type donated the useful term 'bombastic' to language. Paracelsus was, by some measures, a medical progressive who was amongst the first to distinguish between acquired and inherited mental defects – a concept predicting nature and nurture – identified the glandular cause of cretinism and experimented with therapies involving sulphur. All very modern, except at the same time he believed in elves and fairies. But like all successful quacks – indeed, like all successful pitchmen – he spoke a language his audience could understand and found persuasive.

Significantly, Paracelsus' astonishing act of self-promotion has been interpreted differently at different historical moments. Romantically, Shelley thought him a necromancer, while the Nazis admired him for promoting ethnic German folk cures in the German language, rather than lofty Latin. Prince Charles, by way of contrast, has more recently identified this fulminating madman as a pioneering 'alternative healer'.

Charlatans fascinate the literary mind since the mechanics of deceit and the spirit of art are so closely linked: etymologically, 'art' is related to 'artificial'. The great seventeenth-century prose writer Sir Thomas Browne wrote enthusiastically of them and of medical quackery in his *Pseudodoxia Epidemica, or Vulgar Errors* (1646). A superb eighteenth-century charlatan was George Psalmanazar who appeared in London in 1703, apparently a vagrant, claiming to be from Taiwan (then known as Formosa). In powers of deception he exceeded any of the great impostors of learning. At public meetings he ate raw meat and unwashed root vegetables, claiming sensationally that it was Formosan custom annually to sacrifice 18,000 eight-year-old boys and, on a monthly basis, to sacrifice 1,000 beasts (when available) in the country's temples. Although utterly fantastical, general knowledge of Asian manners was imprecise in early-eighteenth-century London and, while Psalmanazar was often questioned and challenged on his outrageous claims, complete repudiation was never demanded nor ever offered. His pitch – well rehearsed, plausibly delivered with charm and passion – was immediately persuasive.

Psalmanazar even published a completely bogus guide to Formosa the following year, an 'illusion eminently bold' according to Isaac D'Israeli. Scholars now know that Psalmanazar's *An Historical and Geographical Description of Formosa* was liberally plagiarized from Varenius' *Descriptio Regni Japoniae et Siam* of the previous century, but this cynical literary theft did not, however, prevent him in later life from becoming a firm friend of a young Dr Johnson, author of the first systematic English dictionary. Johnson said of this preposterous fraud that his 'piety, penitence and virtue exceeded almost what we read as wonderful, even in the lives of the saints'. At about this time Psalmanazar pioneered product endorsement, lending his garish celebrity to the commercialization of an unusual white Japan lacquer. Towards the end of his life Psalmanazar had developed a daily habit of ten spoons of

> **Piety, penitence and virtue exceeded almost what we read as wonderful, even in the lives of the saints**

opium. He requested an unmarked grave, as if this pursuit of anonymity and humility was an act of exculpation from the extravagant deceptions of his life.

Psalmanazar was featured in Isaac D'Israeli's *Curiosities of Literature*, a bestseller of 1824 with its hypnotically fascinating accounts of odd habits and eccentric behaviour among the bookish. The Neapolitan Gemelli Carreri, for example, who although confined to his room by a 'tedious indisposition' was not deterred in his imagination and settled down to write *A Voyage around the World*. Count Cagliostro, another of history's great fraudsters and impostors, was the assumed title and name of one Giuseppe Balsamo, who lived his entire life juggling ideas, selling love philtres and wrinkle creams, relying on the seriousness of his pitch and the credulity of his audience to win the day . . . and save him from jail. Among his many effective frauds was offering everlasting youth to whomsoever would pay for the secret; alas, the pitch materials have been lost. Cagliostro was implicated in an infamous jewel heist involving Marie Antoinette and thus assumed his place in history. Thomas Carlyle wrote a marvellous portrait of him:

> Seasons there may be when Count Proteus-Incognito has his epaulettes torn from his shoulders; his garment-skirts clipt close by the buttocks . . . Harpies of the Law defile his solemn feasts; his light burns languid; for a space seems utterly snuffed out, and dead in malodorous vapour. Dead only to blaze up the brighter! There is scoundrel-life in Beppo Cagliostro; cast him among the mud, tread him out of sight there, the miasmata do but stimulate and refresh him, he rises sneezing, is strong and young again.

In the provision of charlatans, the nineteenth century was not inferior to the eighteenth, although they now began to shade into mainstream commerce and show business (a profession where many remain). The prodigal circus promoter Phineas T. Barnum was typical. Proprietor of 'The Greatest Show on Earth', Barnum was the inspired impresario of Tom Thumb and Jumbo the Elephant, as well as a black woman whom he claimed was 161 years old, but on her death turned out to be merely eighty. Barnum lectured successfully on the 'Philosophy of Humbug', using pseudo-science to help in image building … a stratagem, since widely imitated, that helped make his fortune. Or Dr John Brinkley who, by some estimates, earned $12 million from inject-ing tissues from Toggenberg goats into the prostate gland of ail-ing patients to revivify their sex lives. Then there was the faith healer, carnival hand and seductive evangelist Aimee Semple McPherson, a handsome (and apparently pious) woman undone by lust.

Even the great Victorian engineer Isambard Kingdom Brunel was aware that he had, apart from bridges and boats, to design an image to sell. The famous 1857 photograph of him standing before the launching chains of the *Great Eastern*, so far from being frank reportage of a genius taking a moment off work, may be a deliberate and significant exercise in image-manipulation, one of the very first. This image secured Brunel's status as a romantic, propelling him to number two in TV's popular *Great Briton* charts, shading Shakespeare, with a celebrity only exceeded by Churchill.

The photograph was taken by Robert Howlett, a pioneering professional who died aged twenty-seven, according to legend from over-exposure to primitive and corrosive early photographic chemicals. The picture we know – insouciant, informal, even arrogantly relaxed, with stovepipe hat and cigar, a snapshot of the engineer as hero – was one of three Howlett took of Brunel as part of what we would now call a public-relations campaign, including photos of the ship itself and shipyard reportage.

Brunel had originally asked a colleague to be in the picture, but he declined, leaving the chief engineer as a solo subject. But in 1857 there was no such thing as a snapshot. Before film became commercially available the process of taking a portrait photograph out of doors was arduous and time-consuming: there was a clumsy tripod-mounted camera using glass plates coated with nitrocellulose dissolved in ether and then covered with photo-active silver nitrate. These would be prepared and processed on site in a mobile darkroom. To attempt three different versions of a portrait over several days suggests both photographer and subject were in pursuit of an ideal image.

The first portrait shows Brunel partially seated, with disturbing foreshortening. And he appears to be dominated by those gigantic chains. A second has him in a more commanding standing position, suggesting greater authority. Only in the third portrait were all the elements successfully resolved into the psychologically compelling image we remember.

Binoculars, hat, cigar and mucky boots are artfully arranged

Binoculars, hat, cigar and mucky boots are artfully arranged, while the posture conveys the perfectly judged mixture of swagger and technocratic willpower, a Bohemian in chains, that have made Brunel's reputation.

The very last photograph of Brunel shows how very artful

Howlett's adroitly manipulated photograph was. On the deck of the *Great Eastern* on 5 September 1859, ten days before he died, Brunel is unrecognizable. He has taken his hat off, revealing a bald head. He looks the provincial schoolmaster rather than the international hero; so far from dominating the composition and dominating the ship, he seems hesitant, almost humbled. This insignificant image of Brunel would never have helped its subject to celebrity. Howlett's famous picture, on the other hand, has become a visual eponym for all that was wonderful about Victorian ingenuity. People, by contrast, neither know nor care very much about how Brunel's more conservative contemporary Robert Stephenson looked. How wonderful to reflect that seventy years before a nephew of Freud's invented public relations in New York, a jobbing photographer and an eccentric engineer on a job in Millwall, with their collodion plates and wobbly darkroom, their artful props and their bravura pose, proved that curious truth: with mass media, images are real. Nice to think of Isambard Kingdom Brunel as a pioneer of, among so many other marvellous things, PR.

In his book *Les Fourberies des Charlatans* (Paris, n.d., but appearing in the same series of useful self-help books such as *Pour Rire en Société*), Etienne Ducret summarizes the status of his subject: '*Le domaine du charlatanisme est infini, et sa clientèle innombrable; elle abonde partout ou sont en majorité les crédules et les sots; et où cela n'est-il pas?*' ('The world of charlatanism is infinite and its client base innumerable; it flourishes especially where there is a majority of credulous fools. And where isn't there?')

In the twentieth century, professional deception has not been restricted to circuses, stumps and quack medicine, although since Brunel it has developed really rather vigorously in photography:

from attendances at Politburo meetings with personnel airbrushed in or out according to momentary political priorities, to the raising of the flag at Iwo Jima (Joe Rosenthal's brilliant, but stage-managed, image of the heroism of the US Marine Corps), objective truth has often been the victim of political enhancement. In fact, despite the cliché, few instruments are better suited to dissimulation and deception than the very camera that 'never lies'.

Professional deception has become an elaborate military discipline whose deep structure offers ample stimulus for the student of the pitch. There is no better case study in the science of impression management than the history of camouflage. Like 'sashay' (a side-step derived from '*chasser*', to hunt), the word 'camouflage' from the French slang '*camoufler*', meaning '*cacher et déguiser*' or 'hide and disguise', surreptitiously entered English from French. Camouflage is itself a twentieth-century phenomenon, a direct consequence of new military technologies.

> **The world of charlatanism is infinite and its client base innumerable; it flourishes especially where there is a majority of credulous fools. And where isn't there?**

Observation balloons had been used in the American Civil War, but they were tethered and had limited effect on the nature of conflict, which remained essentially close combat. But new technologies changed the geometry of warfare. The arrival first of machine-guns, then of free-roaming spotter planes, changed the scope and scale of battle. Hitherto, soldiers had been brightly coloured both as a gesture of martial pomp and as an aid to recognition on the battlefield, but when a belt-fed recoil-operated Maxim gun had a range of several hundred yards, high visibility became a dangerous liability more than a fashionable display or an operational convenience for the commanding officer. Early in the First World War French soldiers suffered unusually heavy casualties, partly on account of their bright red trousers. Accordingly, a Section de Camouflage was created in 1915, recruiting stage designers and artists. It happened in Germany too: the painter Franz Marc (who with Kandinsky formed the Blaue Reiter group of Expressionists) designed camouflage for the Kaiser's army.

Camouflage is systematic deception. At first camouflage meant the use of drab colours, to blend with Flanders mud, but soon art and science made this deception more systematic. One of the first conceptual innovations in camouflage happened on a train travelling to the naval base at Devonport on 27 April 1917. Officers were aware that at sea the submarine-launched torpedo had had the same effect as the machine-gun on land: combat could be long-range. Early one morning in an exceptionally cold carriage, Norman Wilkinson, trained as an artist and illustrator, but later a Royal Navy commander, noted in his diary that:

> I suddenly got the idea that since it was impossible to paint a ship so that she could not be seen by a submarine, the extreme opposite was the answer – in other words, to paint her, not for low visibility, but in such a way as to break up her form and thus confuse a submarine officer as to the course on which she was heading.

A brilliant version of contrarian logic, rather like the paradoxical French saying *reculer pour mieux sauter* (retreat in order to advance better). Two days later Wilkinson wrote a formal note to the Admiralty, where his suggestion about intelligent deception was enthusiastically taken up. This led to the dazzle-painting of ships: dramatic geometric disruptive patterns whose association with Futurist art is now clear. A 'Dazzle Section' was established at the Royal Academy and 'Dazzle Officers' worked in naval shipyards. One of them was the English Surrealist painter Edward Alexander Wadsworth, who recorded his work in the dry docks of Liverpool and Bristol in a number of memorable canvases.

Systematic camouflaging of soldiers, or 'land warfare assets', came rather later. True, the British had used khaki (from the Urdu word khak for 'dust') in colonial campaigns up and down the Khyber Pass, but creative design of camouflage material for uniforms goes back only to 1929, when the Italians introduced a beautiful disruptive pattern called *telo mimetico* (literally 'imitative cloth'). And since then the development of camouflage has been a continuous global phenomenon, but one which has been at least as much concerned with national identity for posturing politicians as with environmental disguise for fighting soldiers. Military historian Tim Newark explained in 1996: 'Each new nation looks upon the creation of a camouflage suit as a step towards independence as important as creating its own flag.' Systematic deception has become a part of national identity. In exactly the same way, systematic deception may also have a part to play in personal identity. This military technique has various social equivalents.

Here the Russians have made their own distinctive

contribution to the history of visual disinformation. Count Grigori Aleksandrovich Potemkin had become Catherine the Great's lover in 1774 (only the most notable of a long series), but was soon distracted by the busy task of establishing the port of Sebastopol, planning the ideal city of Ekaterinoslav and generally exposing the wild Crimea with its bandits and other impediments to civilization to the invigorating stimulus of new public works.

On his occasional returns to St Petersburg to brief the Empress and, no doubt, resume his status as her favourite, Potemkin was tempted to talk up progress he had made in civilizing the wilds. His rhetoric was more impressive than his real achievements, so when Catherine planned a site visit up the Dnieper in 1787 (using seven floating palaces created for her exclusive use by Potemkin), the good count found it necessary to adapt dull reality to his brilliant imagery.

> Each new nation looks upon the creation of a camouflage suit as a step towards independence as important as creating its own flag

Grazing cattle were temporarily imported on to the river-banks. Filthy villages were disguised by neo-classical façades in shimmering bright new paint. Catherine was beguiled by gay peasants performing interpretative dances; she was entertained by 200 Amazons, 55,000 pots of burning volatiles spelling out her name, plus 20,000 explosive rockets and unnamed numbers of artificial volcanoes underlined the effect. The jealous Saxon ambassador at St Petersburg, Georg von Helbig, began the whisper that Potemkin, frustrated at the lack of real progress in his modernizing, hid untidy peasants and built pasteboard houses to deceive the Empress. *Von Helbig's Potemkinsche Doerfer*, or 'Potemkin Villages', has been an expression for aggrandizing deceptions ever since. But Catherine the Great had been cheerfully deceived by one of history's greatest pitches.

Of course, the pursuit of effective deception can go to disturbing extremes. Recently, SPETSNAZ, the Russian Special Forces, have developed a speciality of camouflaging eyeballs. But more significant is another technological advance originating east of the Urals. When Ben Rich, an engineer at Lockheed's famous Skunk Works, its highly publicized although allegedly top-secret R&D facility in California's San Fernando Valley, discovered a paper by an obscure Russian telecoms engineer called Pyotr Ufimtsev, it inspired Stealth, the *reductio ad absurdum* of camouflage. There was an old military adage that 'you can't hit what you can't see' and in 'Method of Edge Waves in the Physical Theory of Diffraction' Ufimtsev laid the basis for a technology of irrational shapes, sculptured fractals, weird angles (and semantic menace) that literally made aircraft such as the F-117 Nighthawk invisible.

'You can't hit what you can't see', the definition of the *camouflageur's* art, is a useful principle in any pitch. Camouflage is just the most complete expression of impression management, about how the eye can be deceived and how the mind willingly follows that deception. It gets more sophisticated and more conceptual as technology advances – current military research involves bending light to make things invisible – but there are less scientific methods of making an impression, or, avoiding making a bad one. Chesterfield told his son, 'Be wiser than other people if you can; but do not tell them so.' More recently, David Ogilvy, founder of the Ogilvy & Mather advertising agency and an ocean-going maestro of the pitch, explained with mesmeric precision how to make a favourable impression of yourself and, by extension, how to win any pitch:

1. **When in doubt, confuse the issue.**
2. **Always give gracefully what you know you cannot refuse.**
3. **Be sure to carry a box of matches so if you foul the air in someone's bathroom, you can strike a match to eradicate the bad odour.**

No one called David Ogilvy a charlatan, but he knew the black art of persuasion, as surely as Dazzle camouflage painters knew the perceptual psychology of deception. To write in praise of charlatans is not to elevate intellectual fraud. As the historian of medicine Roy Porter maintained, it would be misleading to suggest that orthodox medicine has always been superior to the snake oil of the quack or charlatan. What in one century or decade was trickery or quackery often gets promoted to professional acceptability in the next; thus Prince Charles and Paracelsus. It did not happen with alchemy and black magic, but it did with osteopathy and aromatherapy.

The story of camouflage teaches impression management as an art form, a sort of perceptual chess: if you cannot avoid detection, choose to confuse. But more significant still, if you cannot be seen, you cannot be a target in the first place. The charlatan and the *camouflageur* both know that deception has its rewards. Marvellous, as well, to think that the Potemkin Villages that have become a byword for deceit and sham...never actually existed, except as an image seen from afar.

SUMMARY

CHARLATANISM AND CAMOUFLAGE

❏ Illusions are persuasive (art and music are not facts).

❏ You can't hit what you can't see.

❏ When in doubt, confuse the issue.

❏ Always give gracefully what cannot be refused.

3 Charm: How to lose with style and grace

'OH! HOW VERY charming!' When someone says this, you know things are going well. I doubt, for example, failed burglars hear it often. No-one calls you charming with a view to insulting, although sometimes it can sometimes be snide, if said in *italics*.

To comment on charm is itself a charming gesture. The person who calls you charming is trying to charm you. And in this mutually enriching reflexiveness, this well-mannered rally of delicate goodwill and fine gestures, lies the fascination inherent in one of the most sophisticated weapons in our battle for attention. If I am charming, I will win. And even if I do not win, I will have lost with style and grace.

Charm is a powerful weapon that is also mysterious, romantic and appealing. It is a subtle, but irresistible, commodity. It beguiles, then overwhelms, but never overwhelms immediately. It only reveals itself slowly. And, continuing its interesting complexities, it is as difficult to define in substance as it is easy to detect in effect.

We know, or soon learn, that charm is a reliably efficient negotiating tool in love or in business. It's a warm and glowing attribute, a winning characteristic. The charmer feels good about himself and makes others want to share that feeling: to make them feel good about themselves. Charm is a multiplier of good feelings.

Charm is not always coincidental, nor accidental. A good measure of what we call charm can, like dentistry or making dry-stone walls, be learnt and applied, as if psychological DIY. Certainly, some people might have helpful characteristics in their DNA: an elegant voice, an open expression, fine posture, a twinkling eye. These may, in one way or another, lend themselves to the display or exercise of charm.

Charm is a multiplier of good feelings.

The same people might instinctively, or, at least without conscious effort, find empathy easy. Empathy is almost always charming. After all, we get the concept from the German *einfuhlung* which, literally, means getting into something; in human terms, to be possessed of the kind of insights which allow an imaginative adventure into someone else's being. Sympathy is much more simple, only feeling along with someone. Some animals display traits that might be thought sympathetic. Empathy belongs to a higher order of being, like dolphins.

All of this might make charm seem effortless. But the aspects of charm which may be consciously learnt rather than accidentally, or coincidentally, acquired require special understanding.

The cultural evidence suggests that seven-tenths of charm is often a highly self-conscious, if imperfectly understood, stratagem. Certainly, there are these fortunate people who have congenital charm, or, at least, are born with a generous measure of its attributes. But there are rather more people who find that a small natural endowment of goodness might readily be parlayed into better and more competitive social technique by deciding to become . . . charming. How does this process of becoming charming work?

Consider your own residue of charm. So, look in the mirror with a glum recognition of terrible personal disappointments in genetic inheritance plus failures in grooming and character, what are the next steps towards becoming a more attractive person? We are talking about an attitude – a way of being, an interaction – that is a lubricant, a fuel, a salve. Charm will give you a presence that others find attractive.

Additionally and very likely, charm will also deliver a slight, but insistent, whiff of erotic possibilities. With charm you can create good situations and extract yourself from bad ones. With charm, you will inspire the envy of men and the interest of women. Or at least most of them, most of the time. No-one hates a charmer, but, then again, not everyone admires him.

Steve Jobs did not suffer from sloth, but he was acquainted with the other Deadly Sins. And he was a flatterer too. Indeed, it now

Charm will give you a presence that others find attractive.

seems clear from a reading of business history that theft and flattery, no less than vision and intolerance, defined the personality of this difficult, but inspired, man.

Jobs, according to his biographer Walter Isaacson, was inclined, when it suited him, to give people the impression that he liked them by 'dishing out insincere flattery to those hungry for it'.

Never mind that this begs the question of exactly what 'sincere flattery' might be, I have been told I am charming. Or, more honestly, that I *can be* so. The 'can be' modification is revealing since it confirms the long suspected presence of an off-switch in the charm cabinet. It also confirms that charm is an active and deployable pitching strategy, more useful in some situations than in others.

Like everything to do with manners, charm can only be understood in context. It is a social weapon to be aimed at specific targets: you cannot be charming to yourself. For example, while I may feel no impulse to be cruelly rebarbative to my bus driver or Deliveroo operative, there are few advantages in laying on the charm in circumstances where I am in their company, or at their mercy. There are times when the least effort will do. (I say 'least effort' because it is hard work to be charming. And if charm looks easy, it is an ease that is hard-won.)

There are circumstances where charm does not work, hence the off-switch. On the other hand, a person I find attractive or a ripe business prospect awaiting a different style of seduction might well discover that I can, indeed, be charming. I become switched on. If I am charming, I am better able to get what I want, or, at least, manoeuvre nearer to it with insincere, or even sincere, flattery.

But since bus routes and postal deliveries are not susceptible to change or persuasion, charm may be wasted on bus drivers and postmen. Charmers may wish to save their lubricant or weapon (the metaphors are as various as the subject) for when it's really needed.

In this way, people can be victims of charm as readily as they can be its beneficiaries. To experience someone's charm is not always to experience benefits. People can fall under charm's spell – and spells, as all shamans and magicians know, can be bad as well as good. Often, charm is misleading. Smarm can be mistaken for charm, just as stupidity can be confused with malice.

At this point it needs to be said that the exercise of charm has something in common with the manipulative stratagems of the psychopath. A good working definition of this catastrophic condition can be found in Hervey M. Checkley's 1941 classic of psychiatry, *The Mask of Sanity*. The motif of the mask immediately suggests disguise and dissimulation in its primary subject matter: the conduct of a good life and its contrast with an aberrant psyche.

Checkley's description of the psychopath can serve as a description of the charmer. The psychopath is someone at once intelligent, unreliable, dishonest, irresponsible, self-centred, shallow and lacking in empathy. The variance is only at the end: charmers have empathy, but in other respects it's a good checklist.

Like the charmer, the psychopath has a method. And each may be, at different parts of the conquest process, persuasive and attractive too. The method has three phases: assessment, manipulation and abandonment. With the psychopath, cruelty and criminal activity are often the end result. The charmer is less damaging, since the victim will feel no hurt greater than that of a temporary seduction, but the process is similar.

First, the charmer finds his victim, either a target of opportunity at a cocktail party or a premeditated one in a business plan. Second, with witty and engaging exchanges, he then exercises his charm in order to achieve his romantic or his professional goals. Third, he then moves on to his next target and the cycle recurs. Recurrence is an important idea here, since people with charm are always restless in wanting to give it exercise. Charm is not idle. It is, and this sounds paradoxical, psychologically aggressive.

What exactly is meant when it is said a man is charming? He has curiosity without being intrusively inquisitive. He has a confident, but not swaggering, bearing that's modified by a sensitive and intelligent reticence in the way he holds himself. He does not sulk, nor does he strut. It's a matter of balance and he finds a physical posture in-between. He engages. He listens. He is empathetic. He has curiosity, is never short of something to say, but he knows the value of a theatrical pause.

The charmer's gentle humour relies on elegant wit rather than clunking jokes. It's a pretty sound rule that jokes are never charming. Still, a charming man is one who laughs at *my* jokes. It makes me feel good that he acknowledges my efforts to be amusing. And a charming man has a sense of balance in all things besides posture. In arguments he knows when to stop. He knows when to leave the party. He's never a bore and while he can, if necessary, be sympathetic, a charmer would never, ever be creepily obsequious. The charmer is a man who leads.

Charm lightens and amuses. It is never heavy, obdurate or fatiguing. Charm is not charm which doesn't change 'when it alteration finds'. People who possess charm know it's a means to get their own way without use of force, at least not of the physical kind. Charm is potent, but subtle. It is one of the oldest and greatest arts of persuasion. And it should be a part of any pitch.

People naturally wish to be sociable, and charm is an accelerant of social success. Pouring drinks, putting guests at their ease, chatting, flirting: these are all charming. Or can be if you are a charming person: a hundred little social gestures which some find automatic, others find impossible. Despite these positive and attractive characteristics, charm is rare.

But the rarity of charm does not always enhance its value. A part of any definition would be that charm is never, at least immediately, repulsive. If you are repelled, you have certainly not had a charming encounter. But, at the same time, charm is not an indisputably positive attribute. People can get hurt by charm: like any contrivance, like any weapon, it can be dangerous if abused.

At this point, consider the idea of lying. Or even the Art of Lying. A charming person may be saying things he knows to be untrue and acting roles he feels to be false. But he will mislead to seduce; charm is more a matter of poetry and theatre than it is of quantifiable strategy. Charming behaviour has only an incidental relationship to objectively observed fact, whatever that it may be. Charm is less obnoxious than an outright lie only because it is less damaging and more elegant.

Charm is less obnoxious than an outright lie only because it is less damaging and more elegant.

Charm may demand a higher – or possibly lower – standard of proof than a lie itself. Lies are on a grey scale that begins with half-truths – a half-truth being something not wholly false, but neither wholly true. Machiavelli, as usual, had a significant point to make: do not bother to use force when deception will do just as well. Why thump someone when you can stroke them? Why confront them when you can charm them? Jean Cocteau said, 'I lie to tell the truth.' You could add that I charm to get my own way.

It was said of Henry Kissinger that he did not lie because it was in his interest, he lied because it was in his nature. He simply could not help himself.

Lies are by no means necessarily charming, even if charm involves equivalent levels of dissimulation and the same desire to mislead or misinform. But charm is superior to lying if only because there is rather less of it around.

Lies are everywhere, while charm is hard to come by and exclusive. There is even a way of measuring lies. One modern authority on fibs, Daniel Nanavati, says in *A Brief History of Lies* (2010) that, as soon as a conversation lasts for more than ten minutes (the same time it takes to notice charm), about twenty per cent of the contents becomes a lie. That figure may well rise in time. Charm, however, is elusive. And because of this, charm is correspondingly powerful.

SUMMARY

CHARM

❑ **Charm can be a powerful weapon.**

❑ **It can often be misleading.**

❑ **Charmers differ from psychopaths in that they have empathy.**

❑ **Charm is one of the oldest and greatest arts of persuasion and should be used in any pitch.**

4 Seduction, or, how to get to yes

LIFE'S GREATEST pitch is a date. And a diagram of sex, with its ascents, peaks, troughs and resulting calm is a diagram of a successful pitch. That is how primal it all is.

Seduction? Flintstone-era lovers needed no guile, only a brontosaurus femur club and pheromones undisguised by industrial deodorants. Do you kneel with a bunch of flowers and look imploring? That's a visual cliché so exhausted that it's not available for ironic re-uptake in even the worst movies. Instead, seduction takes many different forms, although the purpose is always the same: to win someone's body and mind; to influence her, or his, decision-making.

The Journal of Advertising Research recently found that emotions are twice as important as facts in the consumer's decision-making process. And the same principle applies to more intimate relationships. That's the whole essence of this book: communicating your purpose and getting your way, beating your path to 'yes'. Business is more emotional than you first thought, but – equally – your emotional life may benefit from a more businesslike approach. In her essay 'On Not Knowing Greek', from *The Common Reader* (1925) Virginia Woolf (who actually knew Greek rather well) considered the important aspects of existence: 'The interest in life does not lie in what people do, nor even in their relations to each other, but largely in the power to communicate with a third party, antagonistic, enigmatic, yet perhaps persuadable, which one may call life in general.' So, life in general is largely about persuasion, whether commercial, social or sexual. Seduction may, on the face of it, involve only first and second rather than third parties, but its structure and dynamic – that diagram – are relevant to communications as a whole. That diagram could be expressed in imaginative, quantitative graphics: a long flat approach leading to mounting excitement, followed by a critical peak and then a relapse followed by (if all has gone well in bed or business) that period of calm . . . possibly followed by a further slow enlarging of interest.

There is, apart from the graphic representation, very little that is scientific about any form of seduction, although chef Gordon Ramsay advocates buckwheat blinis as part of any menu because it 'will make them feel a lot more fucking healthy' than ordinary flour. But generally, seduction is much more a matter of mood and feeling than of formulas: the aphrodisiac property possessed by oysters is their deliciousness, not any obscure psycho-active agent. For instance, the biological processes aside, there are no facts about sex, although Shakespeare thought lovers and

There are no facts about sex

madmen had much in common: being driven beyond reason by love, or lust, is a recurrent theme in his *Sonnets* and elsewhere. This is a connection later confirmed by the publication in 1843 of the syphilitically deranged Sören Kierkegaard's *Seducer's Diary*. Racked with doubt and anguish, in Jorge Luis Borges's description, Kierkegaard explained there are only desires, frustrations and inspirations, observations and reactions. None of these has a precise numerical character, none can be quantified. But all are felt very keenly, often overwhelmingly strongly, and tend to follow a similar pattern.

The contest between feelings and facts is a defining aspect of contemporary life. This book is about the absolute primacy of feelings, but governments, businesses and their advisers all, alas, tend to disagree. When Alfred McKinsey made his superstitious confession of numerology and its significance in management he created a pernicious, inhumane, Stakhanovite heresy that continues to inspire governments and businesses throughout the West. The idea of measurement being the key to control is 180° wrong. Get a government department or a marketing director to put a number on something and he will convince himself – and perhaps even others – that he understands it. But numbers are only useful guides in banal tasks such as stocktaking how many kitchen rolls you have left in the warehouse in Andover. In all the most important aspects of business, the smouldering desire that leads to an intention to purchase is a powerful force that cannot be turned into a number to be crunched, only a thought to be savoured. And, to turn McKinsey on his head, if it cannot be quantified, it cannot be measured. Just as you cannot hit what you cannot see. Steve Jobs of Apple Computer described his method of approving new products: you know a design is good if you want to lick it. Clearly, at Apple Computer, product development engages the senses before it gratifies the intellect. McKinsey cannot evaluate, measure and manage licking, although the seducer most certainly can. And we can learn from him.

You know a design is good if you want to lick it

There are two aspects of seduction. The first is the brute bending of another individual's will to your own, the better to gratify your desires. The second is the catalogue of carnal and sensory delectations that are the result, at least in theory, of successful seduction. Seduction is inherently exploitative; it does not occur between equals, but the balance of power can shift in surprising ways during the process. Experts seem to agree that subtlety is more likely to bring results than a brutal approach. As Kierkegaard's Johannes character notes in *The Seducer's Diary*: 'I do not approach her, I merely skirt the periphery of her existence . . . This is the first web into which she must be spun.'

Curiously, the early Church was well informed on each aspect of seduction, the physical and the metaphysical. While St Thomas Aquinas held that any expression of lust was a mortal sin, he had more liberal contemporaries who argued that it was perfectly fine to stroke someone's hand or, I suppose, knee, provided only that no sexual frisson was experienced. One imagines with amusement the exhaustive behavioural experiments in the monasteries and nunneries to determine just where ordinary pleasure ended and erotic enlightenment began. We know now that the madness of love is a function of the presence of PEA, or phenylethylamine, which stimulates infatuation. In the past, they perforce used less scientific measures. A McKinsey consultant might show an amorous target a bar chart attached to a clipboard. John Donne would whisper imaginative poetry, including one uniquely marvellous line containing only prepositions:

Licence my roving hands, and let them go,
Before, behind, above, between, below.

Seduction, because it involves a change of status between two people, shares the structural dynamic of a pitch and pleading is often involved. As John Donne had it:

Come, madam, come, all rest my powers defie
Until in labour, I in labour lie

It is a primal case of before-and-after, with a gradient, and any seduction is always a challenge to and change of the established order. Hence there have always been strictures against it. Gregory the Great insisted that anybody who seduced a virgin should either marry her or do penance in a monastery after a sound thrashing. If a virgin was seduced by deception, then the option existed for the seducer to provide a dowry, if unprepared to marry. Here, the definition of deception is specially interesting. At this time the Church's conception of lust held women to be damaged or devalued by the exercise of it, hence the insistence on reparations to be made by the suitor. It was to be a millennium or so before Gloria Steinem would write, 'Power can be taken, but not given. The process of the taking is empowerment in itself.'

Although seduction is by no means wholly a matter of sexual adventure, its erotic aspects have a fine metaphorical relevance to seduction in all its forms.

> **Clothing is essentially erotic since to disguise something is, in effect, to draw attention to it.**

And it is all about appearances and how they persuade us. As Alison Lurie explained in *The Language of Clothes* (1981), clothing is essentially erotic since to disguise something is, in effect, to draw attention to it. This instinct for concealment was often observed by early travellers to the South Seas and it often had a contradictory character.

Many 'primitives' accustomed to going naked nonetheless had keen senses of modesty and propriety, not to say style. The well-dressed New Hebridean man would have his penis bound in calico up to two feet in length and two inches in diameter, supported upwards by means of a belt. Its extremity would be decorated with flowering grasses, although his testicles would be left exposed. In Tahiti, Captain Cook found the aboriginals unabashed to 'gratify every appetite and passion before witnesses', yet restrained by other proprieties. Some travellers in the Middle East in the nineteenth century found that naked women disturbed when bathing would instinctively cover their faces, not their bodies.

In contrast, Western experience has evolved more rigorous codes of modesty, perhaps the better to satisfy the devils of lust. Since modesty tends to excite passion, it is rueful to consider what effect immodesty might have. That seduction is easier in the dark is a classical idea, attributed by Burton in the *Anatomy of Melancholie*

Shyness, or at least indifference, seems a powerful stimulus to seduction

(1621) to Dandinus, who wrote '*nox facit impudentes*'. Anthony Burgess described the *Anatomy* as 'by a magnificent and somehow very English irony, one of the great comic works of the world'. Shyness, according to Restif de la Bretonne's scabrous autobiographical *Monsieur Nicolas* (1794–7) is no more than a premature consciousness of sex. The confessionals of Restif de la Bretonne and Casanova were, incidentally, both cited by erotomaniac

Henry Miller as books he was disappointed never to have read.

Indeed, shyness, or at least indifference, seems a powerful stimulus to seduction. In *The Young Hitler I Knew* (1954) August Kubizek speculated on what made women want to seduce the Führer, as many apparently did. Considering first his bright eyes, then his stern expression, he decided that what was, after all, the basis of Hitler's attractiveness was his complete lack of interest. Ambitious seducers wanted to test it. As an aside to this note about the attractiveness of Hitler, Dorothy Parker's requirements in a man she wished to seduce were that he should be 'handsome, ruthless and stupid'.

The art of seduction was brought to a quite exceptional height of refinement by Casanova, a friend of Voltaire, occultist, traveller and historian. He treated his life as theatre, moving around the courts and boudoirs of Europe with a trunk of fans, jewels, props and gifts. By his own, perhaps unreliable, account he enjoyed a total of 122 women, fewer than Don Giovanni's 1,003, but nonetheless splendid inspiration for a marvellous book. Casanova wrote wonderfully about his art and a close analysis of his technique in wooing is instructive to the pitchman. Casanova would study his target and empathize with her changing moods. He would find out what was missing from her life and then satisfy both herself and, eventually, himself. It is a simple routine to win a person's attention . . . and one that is recommended today by motivational speakers. Casanova would also

> In the course of a single night he wrote an entire play without using the letter 'r' in order to impress (and then seduce) an actress who suffered from a lisp.

go to painstaking efforts to win his pitch. In the course of a single night he wrote an entire play without using the letter 'r' in order to impress (and then seduce) an actress who suffered from a lisp.

But nor was he without deception and trickery. The elderly Marquise d'Urfe wished to become a young man. Casanova was reluctant to refuse the brief of this influential *patronne* so persuaded her that she might propitiate the Spirit of the Moon (apparently influential in the matters of sex-change and time travel) by hurling a chest of jewels into the ocean. This was done, whereupon Casanova purloined the booty and made off with it. His *Memoirs* (only published in 1960) are beautiful and affecting. In them he says he never considered repentance, because you only repent crimes, not pleasures.

The fascination of seduction is that it entails consent. Without consent, the process would end in something ugly called rape. But some definitions of it are revealing. As recently as 1981 J. M. V. Bowner could write in *Vive la Différence* that rape is a 'perfectly natural function'. To agree with that statement requires a disagreeable understanding of what constitutes 'natural', but even the finest minds have found a curious ambiguity in the matter of sex without consent.

The great Cambridge psychiatrist Anthony Storr published his book *Sexual Deviation* in 1964. In it he writes:

The idea of being forcibly overpowered by a male must have occurred to every woman at some time, although not all women recognise that the apprehension to which such thoughts give rise is not unmixed with pleasure. The situation of being overpowered by a male is also one in which permission is given to be erotic, since the victim is forced to comply. Thus she 'cannot help it' and can enjoy the thrill without incurring either blame or responsibility.

For his part, the novelist Norman Mailer pugnaciously declared at a 1972 UCLA speech 'a little bit of rape is good for man's soul', thus unconsciously confirming the selfish primacy of fact-driven, phallocentric male logic which has done so much to stimulate the hordes of the militant feminists. On the other hand, let it be noted that the Vakuta women of Melanesia rape their menfolk as a matter of custom. Notions of consent may define the art of seduction, but they also offer important insights into the structure of a pitch. While you can rarely bore someone into saying yes, ingenuity may have only a limited effect.

Doris Langley Moore was an extraordinary Liverpudlian woman. With a background in the theatre, she designed the costumes for John Huston's production of *Freud*. Her book (the first edition was anonymous) *The Technique of the Love Affair* (1926) is at the same time sexually, socially and psychologically precocious.

Morals of the day required a degree of subterfuge, so Moore ingeniously structures her book as an exchange of letters between two inquisitive women, the one more experienced than the other. In their correspondence we can

Well-adjusted people, Freud argued, had lots of guilt-free and satisfying sex

see the emotional graph of the love affair and calculate its equivalence to the dynamics of a sound business relationship.

One correspondent, Cypria, writes: 'A successful love affair is one which results either in permanent mating or in mutual friendship, and for this nothing is more efficacious than to inspire in your subject an admiration kept so perpetually alert that it almost reaches the high pitch of infatuation, but does not quite . . .' This policy of *coitus reservatus* may be sexually unsatisfactory, but has some clear advantages in business.

Freud's Seduction Theory is fascinating not so much for its contents (a rather aberrant notion that most psychiatric disorders were caused by repressed memories of child abuse), but because his creation, prosecution and ultimate abandonment of a slightly potty hypothesis powerfully illuminates the impressive methods of this master of persuasion. To sell his theories Freud used intellectual deceptions, although they masqueraded as value-free science.

Originally, Freud had believed that aggression was the source of human motivation, but in the course of interviewing disturbed patients he came to decide that it was sex. Freud's reputation for understanding everything about sex was so widespread by 1924 that Sam Goldwyn, not a bookish man, offered him $100,000 to consult on a movie treatment about great lovers in history. This offer Freud declined.

Sex provided for Freud what he called the 'indispensable "organic foundation"' of behaviour: the universality and the obviousness of sex had clear appeal to an entrepreneurial scientist intent on seducing the public into believing he was right. Well-adjusted people, Freud argued, had lots of guilt-free and satisfying sex, arriving at the state which Anthony Storr described as 'tensionless Nirvana'. People who were not well adjusted, namely his patients, had been damaged by their seduction when a child by an adult, usually of a daughter by a father. Repressing this traumatic experience drove you to the consulting couch.

Eventually, Richard Webster explained in his iconoclastic book *Why Freud Was Wrong* (1995) that the psychoanalytic method involved 'completely speculative allegations', based on patient confessions not always given honestly or freely. Thus, one of the great hypotheses in modern thought was based on cod data, wilfully manipulated to close a circular argument. Freud was forced to abandon Seduction Theory because:

1. **There was surely no valid correlation between the statistics of neurosis and the reality of child abuse.**
2. **Since his own siblings displayed neurotic symptoms, Freud would have been forced to accept that his father had been a child abuser.**
3. **During one of his routine periods of self-analysis, Freud realized that his own preoccupation with incest was based on an incestuous fantasy (he admitted some erotic interest in seeing his mother naked) and so, therefore, must many of his patient 'confessions' have been fantasy too.**

But whatever your position vis-à-vis Freud's Seduction Theory, whatever the position of your knee with respect to the carpet, seduction is a fundamental part of the commerce of existence. Few of us are, alas, in a position to follow Chesterfield's advice to his son too literally. 'Make love', he wrote, 'to every beautiful woman you meet ... and just be gallant with the rest', but as an idea it has an attractive permanence ... even if it assumes, as most pitches do, an element of cynicism.

SUMMARY

SEDUCTION

❏ Emotions are more persuasive than facts.

❏ Classic management theory is wrong: the most important things can neither be measured nor managed.

❏ Seduction is disruptive.

❏ You cannot bore someone into saying 'yes'.

5 How to write a letter

No MATTER what the medium, paper or electrons, a letter is one of the most powerful devices in any pitch. How best to write effective ones? Should love letters be badly written to demonstrate sincerity? James Joyce seems to have thought so. Writing to his wife Nora Barnacle, the author of Ulysses (which, at 22,000 words, contains the most rambling sentence in the English language) expressed himself like a staccato fumbling schoolboy: 'When I am with you I leave aside my contemptuous, suspicious nature. I wish I felt your head on my shoulder. I think I will go to bed.' Certainly, there is a small history of poets believing an artful carelessness conveys passion with more conviction than cool detachment. Robert Herrick wrote:

A careless shoe-string, in whose tie
I see a wild civility;
Do more bewitch me than when Art
Is too precise in every part.

First the telegram, then the telephone, then fax, now e-mail, text and social media have usurped the everyday role of the letter. No one, as Frank Kermode explained in his *Oxford Book of Letters* (1995) writes to coal merchants any more. No one even has a coal merchant.

For several centuries we have been seduced by the myth of technological progress. Of ever more, ever newer stuff giving us ever more possibilities to make more money, travel more quickly or have better sex. Or, ideally, all of them. But the poisonous, rising tide of digital novelty will soon retreat, driven back by our repugnance about the terrible predicament new technology has created. Yes, we can instantaneously send anyone anywhere on earth our latest video of a surfboarding hamster or buy an artisan pizza on-line.

But at what price? Research has been undermined; newspapers, magazines and books have been devalued or destroyed. Cinema will be soon be ruined. Sex has become trashy commerce. Romance is an electro-chemical dance. Momentary celebrity bests enduring fame. Truth has been relativized, while airborne robots will monitor our every activity and smartphones betray us hourly. Uber knows more about us than our parents did. A more connected world is becoming an uglier, more brutish world.

So what values will we be left with when the corrosive digital tide begins to retreat? It's time to discover and explain that analogue is better than digital. Stuff is better than bytes;

maps are better than sat-nav;
flirting is better than Tinder;
postcards are better than Instagram;
style is better than fashion;
history is better than futurism;
privacy is better than connectivity;
vinyl is better than Spotify;
letters are better than e-mail.

All of this is true. And it proves that humane values including privacy and charm are becoming increasingly valuable.

Technology has achieved instantaneous, soulless efficiency ... something 'too precise in every part'. E-mail is a cold convenience and a hot curse. Too many and you feel put-upon. Not enough and you feel neglected. We are now beginning to understand that social media can be disturbingly manipulative, as much as it can be liberating. And, as in sex and food, with letters slow is better than fast. Nancy Mitford thought air mail showed an ungentlemanly sense of urgency. E-mail is intrusive, peremptory and demanding, if addictive. And something about it – perhaps the immediacy – seems positively to inhibit literacy and elegance. In any case, e-mail will soon be replaced by something even more hellishly peremptory.

But the personal letter – intimate and lasting – has a different quality to electronic bit-spit: as Dr Johnson knew, 'In a man's letters . . . his soul lies naked.' That is part of its attraction and its challenge. When a distressed Machiavelli was effectively a captive of the Franciscans at Carpi, he often wrote three times a day to his friend Francesco Guicciardini.

And the letter may just be ready for a revival. Its humane values are very sympathetic to the spirit of an age where in all fields of consumer activity there's increasing evidence that people want quality of experience, not quantity of it. Jane Austen, thinking of love letters, said, 'There is a time in one's life when the Post Office has deep significance.' That's what letters are all about: human relations made concrete . . . on paper or on the screen.

Twenty years ago the inheritors of Jane Austen's Post Office had a project to double the volume of what, in the mincing language of the bureaucrat, it called the 'social letter'. Achieving a 'better-balanced doormat' was not only an attractive cultural objective for that great majority bored and irritated by intrusive junk mail, but also a compelling commercial objective. In deserts of polchrome rubbish, real letters – by which we mean real messages from individual people, not arid business communications – stand out like the most lush and tempting oasis. Only the dullest person or most irrecoverable cynic is not excited to discover a personal letter among the bills, pizza fliers, airport taxi service biz cards and circulars. Why? Because the letter is an art form that's democratically and cheaply available to the 98 per cent of the population who are literate.

So how do you write one?

Well, you can safely ignore the advice of the popular word-processing software. Both Microsoft and Apple offer hilariously inept letter templates, awful beyond the scope of even ironic detachment. MSWord offers a 'Dear Mom' example, while Appleworks has an 'Apology' template, with tips on how the computer-dependent epistolic stylist might customize his efforts the better to achieve a sense of authentic personality. Other people's letters always make very good reading . . . except, of course, when they are computer-generated. Better to follow the masters. In her autobiography *A Far Cry from Kensington* (1988) Muriel Spark said of her novels: 'You are writing to a friend. Write privately, not publicly, without fear or timidity.' Exactly the same applies to letters. If you can speak it, write it.

The novelist and critic Frank Delaney had a ten-point list for writing fiction which applies, with some small modifications, to letters.

1. Choose your setting carefully (or: make sure you have something to say).

2. Like your characters (or: be certain you want to amuse, delight or possibly even seduce your correspondent).

3. It is 90 per cent perspiration (or: you have to be prepared to make an effort).

4. Write from experience (or: effective letter-writing is not about ambitious literary conceits, rather the simple and accurate description of feelings and experiences).

5. Let your imagination go (or: don't be afraid to go on imaginative detours).

6. Know your reader (or: make an effort to be interesting).

7. Be entertaining (or: be funny).

8. Study the classics (or: you can never have too many good examples to inspire and instruct).

9. Know your limits (or: humble authenticity is always more attractive than vaulting pretension).

10. Make it new (or: nothing is ever quite so compelling as an original, first-hand account of an experience).

History offers us four major types of letter, still relevant today. The love letter; the complaint; job applications or personal statements and goodbyes. Classics of these genres are, in order, Tchaikovsky to his patron, Nadejda von Meck; Dr Johnson to Lord Chesterfield; Leonardo da Vinci to the Duke of Milan and Beethoven's haunting 'Heiligenstadt Testament'. This is how they worked.

The love letter

Nadejda von Meck was a widowed aristocrat, the mother of eighteen children (eleven of whom survived), who fell in love with the gay composer when she heard Nicolai Rubinstein play his 'Tempest'. Their correspondence began in 1876, although each decided not to meet the other. She supported him both personally (through a doomed marriage to a pupil at the Conservatoire) and financially (she gave him an annuity of six thousand roubles, a compliment he returned by dedicating his Fourth Symphony to her). Until she ended the correspondence (and annuity) in 1890, their letters were one of the most bizarre and intimate correspondences of history. Against her apparently cool detachment, Tchaikovsky wrote with a penetrating intimacy. A typical letter begins: 'It is impossible to say how glad I was to see your handwriting,' thus immediately confirming their closeness and demanding that the reader read on. A middle paragraph describes 'the deepest and most secret gropings of my soul', exciting in the reader a delicious voyeurism about revelations to come. The same letter ends with a touching imprecation, simply expressed: 'I desire for you a spirit of well and calm.' Intimacy, self-revelation and empathy made Tchaikovksy a great letter-writer. This was written exactly as he might have spoken.

> It is impossible to say how glad I was to see your handwriting

The complaint

A letter Dr Johnson wrote to the Earl of Chesterfield has been described by Thomas Carlyle as a 'Blast of Doom' and is usually said to be the most famous single letter in English literature. It is certainly the best complaint. The circumstances of its writing are marvellously evocative of master–slave relationships, of the pride of a poor author confronting the condescension of the privileged grandee, of revenge through writing.

Johnson began writing – 'amidst inconvenience and distraction, in sickness and in sorrow' – his great Dictionary in 1747. He pitched a prospectus to Chesterfield, with a view to acquiring patronage (against the prospect of the Dictionary carrying a dedication to its sponsor). Accordingly, Chesterfield patronized him with the gift of ten pounds. This infuriated Johnson so that, even after seven years' unsupported work on the Dictionary, when Chesterfield eventually and rather grandly offered support, his lordship's offer was rejected. In the published Dictionary a patron is defined as one 'who supports with insolence and is repaid by flattery', but in the famous letter of 7 February 1755 Johnson has a more stinging definition still: 'Is not a Patron, my Lord, one who looks with unconcern on a man struggling for life in the water, and, when he has reached ground, encumbers him with help?'

> **Is not a Patron, my Lord, one who looks with unconcern on a man struggling for life in the water, and, when he has reached ground, encumbers him with help?**

Johnson's weakness in giving in to the temptation for revenge was more than adequately compensated by his supreme mastery in the use of English. Whether he achieved his aim of wounding Chesterfield we do not know (his lordship did not deign to reply, although did concede that Johnson's letter was 'very well written'), but his technique depended on an elaborate courtesy in address which barely disguises a seething contempt; on a genius for significant imagery and on a beautifully crafted understatement – 'I had exhausted all the art of pleasing which a retired and uncourtly scholar can possess' – more deadly because it is less obvious. Understatement, Johnson knew, reaches a deeper and more sensitive part of the psyche than extravagance or excess.

The job application or personal statement

One of the most significant pitches we make is, as Leonardo da Vinci knew, a job application. The definition of this now blurs with the requirement students have to write a 'personal statement', a sort of advertisement for themselves. As in the other arts and sciences, Leonardo was a master of the pitch. Although Leonardo now enjoys a reputation as a universal genius of unmeasurable celebrity, like Dr Johnson fame did not come to him until his late maturity and even then his professional life was a struggle, leaving him with a measure of disenchantment with his fellow men, especially his temperamental clients, the Medici. Still, his prodigal genius was motivated by his motto of 'obstinate vigour'. Aged thirty Leonardo had become dismayed by the corruption and decadence of his native Florence and wrote a job application and personal statement to Lodovico Sforza, the Duke of Milan, a city with a more businesslike reputation than frivolous and pleasure-loving Florence. His letter begins with an elegant put-down of the competition, saying that his rivals' 'inventions' are nothing of the sort, but are much the same as existing machines in common use. Then, crucially, at the end of his first paragraph, he offers an irresistible tease. Give me an interview, Leonardo says, and I will tell you my secrets.

His letter then goes on a breathless, boggling itinerary, itemizing his accomplishments as a military consultant and contractor. Leonardo says he can:

- ❏ Design light, strong, portable bridges
- ❏ Manage both military and civil waterworks
- ❏ Demolish fortresses
- ❏ Design long-range ordnance (with decorative effects, if required)
- ❏ Engineer tunnels
- ❏ Design tanks
- ❏ Design unsinkable armoured ships
- ❏ Design public buildings and palaces

If these, the letter suggests, are accomplishments he is prepared to put on paper, what war-mongering duke could possibly resist the advantages offered by privileged access to this same entrepreneur's mysterious 'secrets'? Lodovico Sforza could not. He promptly gave Leonardo a job he kept for sixteen years.

And the clincher in Leonardo's letter? Having listed in bathetic style his engineering and design skills, as an almost apologetic footnote he adds (I paraphrase):

'And, oh yes, by the way, I am also a better painter and sculptor than anybody else you care to mention.'

With a mixture of scrupulous over-statement and managed understatement, together with a judicious measure of flattery, dismissal of the competition and the promise of 'secrets to be revealed if you take up this offer', Leonardo wrote one of history's best job applications.

The goodbye letter

This is a curious genre with fewer obvious contemporary applications than the other examples, although it is the one calling for the most determined stripping of the soul. Thus there is none requiring more accurate self-revelation. And there is none more emotive than Beethoven's Heiligenstadt Testament.

Heiligenstadt was the Austrian village where Beethoven holidayed in 1802, just as he was struggling to come to terms with the shocking reality of his increasing deafness. At first the calamity of his musical genius being thwarted by such a cruel impairment caused him to despair, even to consider suicide. But his Heiligenstadt Testament (addressed to his brothers, but never sent and, exactly as Beethoven intended, discovered posthumously and then widely published) describes how through sheer will-power he defied a dismaying affliction.

It was a letter to his brothers, to himself and to the future, setting down in the frankest terms, but without self-pity, the initial crushing embarrassment of a composer having to admit to deafness. He describes how his disability caused, first, social isolation which was misinterpreted as curmudgeonliness. But Beethoven explained: 'I must live like an exile, if I approach near to people a hot terror seizes upon me.' Yet the Testament continues to negotiate the terms and conditions with which Beethoven dealt with Fate. Forced to become a philosopher in addition to being a busy composer, Beethoven explains how he must exist in a state of 'endless suffering' which, exasperatingly, no one will be able to understand until after his death. 'At least,' he writes, 'the world may become reconciled with me after my death.'

> I must live like an exile, if I approach near to people a hot terror seizes upon me.

Indeed it did. At the time he wrote this distraught confessional Beethoven was only working on his Second Symphony, cheerful music entirely at odds with his mood, which Hector

Berlioz described as 'a ravishing picture of innocent pleasure'. Beethoven lived for another twenty-five years and composed his greatest music after writing a letter in which he confesses to have abandoned hope, to be reconciled to a joyless existence sustained not by friends and society, but only by the frustration of composing music he could never hear, except in the scores he performed in his head.

Beethoven's astonishing Heiligenstadt Testament has its equivalent today in the letters many therapists recommend writing to relieve the painful grievances of bereavement: commit to paper your most intimate thoughts, the ones that perhaps most embarrass you, and seal them away in an envelope. Perhaps, the therapists say, take the letter to a beautiful spot and burn it. This, therapists maintain in their own language, creates a pleasing sense of 'closure'. In writing a letter about his most intimate self, but addressed to a future that he would not know, Beethoven achieved that same sense of closure . . . and successfully pitched a version of his life as tormented, but principled, genius that is now a fundamental part of cultural history.

Can't come, a lie by way of excuse follows

But after writing a letter, there is the question of the reply. Andrew Carnegie, the robber baron steel magnate, had splendid advice on how to guarantee a response. His sister-in-law had been troubled by her sons being away at university and never, in the days before phones of one sort or another were a universal convenience, bothering to contact her. Carnegie's solution was to write to his nephews, adding as a PS that he was including a five-dollar bill, something which, in fact, he neglected to do. By return of post he got two replies beginning 'Dear Uncle Andrew . . .' Self-interest ever plays a part in a successful letter. And so, often, does brevity. When bothered by unwanted invitations Marcel Proust's Guermantes used to send a postcard saying: '*Impossible venir, mensonge suit*' ('Can't come, a lie by way of excuse follows'). While not exactly a letter, Abraham Lincoln's 1863 Gettysburg Address – in which he describes the entire past and future moral circumstances of the United States of America – is a mere 264 words. By way of contrast, this paragraph alone is 183 of them.

Letters are a primal form of pitch and it is not just the content but the form that offers considerable scope for self-expression. In a bright and busy world of instantaneous, pixellated, electronic data transmission – broadband, D-RAM, iPod, FireWire, Airport, GSM, GPS, DVD, HDTV, Snapchat and IDGAS (I don't-give-a-stuff) – handwriting is making a comeback. Not that it ever entirely went away. At the height of Wall Street's infatuation with whizz-o automated systems, one bank had stationery printed which carried the rubric 'This message has been handwritten to save time'.

But you don't handwrite a letter to save time, you handwrite to make an impression, as part of your pitch. And it is always favourable. It's *le monde à l'envers*: an address exquisitely printed in Helvetica 12 pt by a computer can be cheerfully ignored. Something written by hand demands attention: it promises intimacy, romance, mystery, opportunity. And the handwriting counts.

There's a clear hierarchy here. A

You don't handwrite a letter to save time, you handwrite to make an impression

letter written in pencil would be very curious. Blue Biro, an insult. One of those Japanese 0.1 mm rollerballs entirely acceptable. But best of all is a fountain pen. Now other hierarchies emerge, initially the colour of the ink. Ancient prejudices are entirely correct: people who use green, brown or purple ink are very likely to be among the criminally insane. Blue ink is, normally, restricted to the very elderly. Black is best. A useful tip on visiting a foreign city: buy a bottle of ink as a rapid introduction to local culture.

Handwriting matters because we live in a world where gestures are increasingly important. Handwriting costs nothing; there is no downside and it is brilliant, free PR. Tom Wolfe knows this: he specializes in an amazingly elaborate signature, like the witnesses on a Tudor legal document. Sir Nikolaus Pevsner, the famed architectural historian, on the other hand, advertised his precision and scholarliness by writing in minuscule. It is worth practising a personal style: when women say, 'You have beautiful handwriting,' it's much sexier than: 'Do you want a good time, big boy?'

Letters are both an advertisement and a camouflage. In crafting a letter, even in crafting an e-mail (where it's vital to attempt literacy and punctuational precision), we create disguises for ourselves. While Oscar Wilde noted 'Man is least himself when he talks in his own person', US journalist Maureen Dowd says she is not at her best in person, but finds it 'easier to be myself when I write'. Julie Burchill says speech is only her second language.

Here is the true appeal of the letter against the grim reality of a flawed personality: a letter preserves and projects and records the very best you can offer. The medium, paper or electronic, filters out the bad moods and the bad hair and the mediocrity of day-to-day existence. A well-crafted letter allows wit and precision to be your representatives and agents. Style and spelling and good paper, a decent pen and black ink make you flawless, or, at the very least, a better version of yourself.

If you must use e-mail, make sure something arresting appears in the subject field. And 'arresting' should not be confused, at least not nowadays, with obscenity: e-mails announcing enhanced sperm integrity or the social felicities offered by a larger penis or the availability of one-legged Russian hookers are mondain and easily ignored. I find 'prat' works well since the receiver neither knows whether this is an accusation or an admission and curiosity leads to investigation. No point sending any message unless it gets noticed.

But old-fashioned letters always work better. A blank piece of paper is the place for a perfect pitch.

SUMMARY

HOW TO WRITE A LETTER

- ❏ Handwriting is powerfully intimate: use a good pen, black ink and decent paper.
- ❏ Make sure you have something to say.
- ❏ Be funny (this takes effort).
- ❏ Mix outrageous over-statement with nice understatement.
- ❏ In an e-mail or a text message, use proper punctuation.

6 Lunch: theory and practice

'HE WAS', I found myself scribbling on the pack of 5 x 3 white cards that accompanies me everywhere, but especially to lunch, 'three packs of grissini late.' The reference is to those annoying, cellophane-wrapped packets of frangible, tasteless Torinese industrial breadsticks which Italian restaurants supply to desiccate customers' mouths in order to encourage enhanced consumption of extravagantly marked-up *acqua minerale* or chalky but quaffable Pinot Grigio. Their subsidiary function is to supply the customer-host with some displacement activity to engage mind and body and palate while waiting for an infuriatingly late guest. Terrible to appear lonely and bereft in a restaurant.

Besides, it's a status thing. Exactly how does the hierarchy of arrivals and delays work? What are the perhaps unconscious distinctions we make which, on some occasions, require us to be punctual and, on others, leave us relaxed or even contemptuous about time-keeping? Could you publish a league with figures attached about allowable degrees of lateness so as to categorize all your potential lunch partners as if in a handicap system? For instance, I would not be late for lunch with Princess Caroline of Monaco (although I would also be at pains not to be too early lest an undignified eagerness be detected), but I wouldn't mind keeping my accountant waiting. In fact, I would very deliberately keep my accountant waiting because to appear too available would be to appear damagingly insignificant and without superior or even simply more profitable distractions.

Anyway, there are about eight grissini to a pack and they are difficult to eat, so someone who is three packs late is teetering on the edge of social acceptability. Someone who is three packs of grissini late is telling you (s)he is either hopelessly disorganized or, perhaps worse, has categorized you as a very low-priority target. But at exactly what stage of lateness do you abandon the prospect of lunch, make your shrugging apologies to the maître d' and leave your annoyingly tardy guest to face the abrupt consequences of his or her arrogant carelessness? There are a few principles. First, you never ever want to be early, especially if you are a guest. To be early suggests an unattractive availability. But if you happen to arrive first, there is only one dignified answer to the question 'Do you want to wait at the bar?' No, you will risk the grissini and wait at the table. To wait at the bar says you are a drinker with time on your hands.

To wait at the bar says you are a drinker with time on your hands.

But the allowable degree of lateness? In big cities, routine delays and obstructions mean people are often ten minutes late. There should be slack in the system to accommodate this sort of reality, but – on the other hand – never trust anyone who blames 'traffic' as if 'traffic' is a surprise event whose hitherto unanticipated consequences have been uniquely focused on the delayed individual. But, whether you are guest or host, does it look pitiable to be prepared to wait for more than half an hour? I think so. I once, through a restaurant window, saw my guest's Porsche looking for a parking place thirty-five minutes after we were meant to meet and I decided to make my excuses before he found a meter.

I was musing these fine thoughts, scribbling again on my 5 x 3s through a moonscape of breadstick crumbs, when the waitress interrupted with the trill 'Still or fizzy?'

Lunch is exercise, mating, dialogue, training. It's a culture with a discipline all its own. Lunch is not for wimps, lunch is for manipulation. Nutrition is of little relevance: there are very good sandwich shops to satisfy brute hunger. Working lunch is a tautology; at the level where people say 'Let's have lunch' you have already begun a work contract . . . and your pitch should be in preparation.

It starts with assessing the candidate. Not everyone is suitable and it is essential to appreciate the different status and differing motives of the luncher and the lunchee. Each role requires different stratagems. A PR will invite you to lunch to enthuse you about a new prospect or client. Always be cautious when invited to a suspiciously expensive restaurant and the conversation turns to business too early. Your brains are going to be picked, although anybody crass enough to use that dire expression of exploitation does not deserve to have invitations accepted in the first place. Another category of lunch is the mutually agreeable escapology between friends. Routine here is to invent, a glass or two after orders have been placed, a system for making millions . . . which turns to dust in the daylight.

As suggested above, lunch with accountants should happen only under duress or if conventional politeness insists, after a financial year of some achievement, you make a gesture of generosity and amiability. While the sign-off on the phone or at a party which goes 'We really must meet for lunch' often actually translates as 'Fuck off, I never want to see you again', the selection of real candidates for lunch is full of nuances and submerged meanings. You only ask someone to lunch if they follow those basic laws of human interaction outlined earlier:

1. **Do they make you laugh or think or are they in a position to tell you something you need to know?**
2. **Are they sexually interesting?**
3. **Are they in a position to give you money?**

Whatever the answers, the thing about lunch is this: you are not paying a hundred pounds (including service) for a cargo cult approximation of *bucatini alla matriciana* followed by *costoletta di maiale alla griglia con spinaci e fagioli*. That would be stupid. You are paying a hundred pounds for the opportunity to make a pitch.

Lunch is a recent phenomenon, unlike dinner, which is more traditional. It is worth noting the following, not least because it may provide useful conversational cues if ever in difficulties in a restaurant. William the Conqueror dined at nine a.m., Henry VII at eleven. To La Rochefoucauld (1613–1680), 'morning' was whatever portion of the day, irrespective of the clock, that occurred before you sat down at table. Sir Richard Steele (1672–1729) noted that 'in my memory, the dinner hour has crept from twelve o'clock to three.' In *Northanger Abbey* General Tilney dines at five (but this is in the country). In the time of Thackeray and Dickens, the dinner hour migrated from six to just before eight. Here it has stayed, although a hellish refinement in conventions now makes people say 'eight for eight-thirty'. In the first edition of Mrs Beeton's great book (1859) a mere eight and a half lines are devoted to lunch, but 251 dinner menus are helpfully provided. This is telling us something about the habits of the mid-nineteenth century. As a professional and commercial rite, if not as a social ritual, lunch has usurped the dinner party as a means to ease the socialization of the middle classes, while offering subtle opportunities for self-promotion or touting for new business under the acceptable camouflage of eating out.

You are paying a hundred pounds for the opportunity to make a pitch.

All that migratory activity by the dinner hour left the middle of the day available for lunch. Timing is easier than dinner. Lunch is always at one. An earlier invitation means your host wants to get away early. A later one means the restaurant does not take you seriously. Of course, the venue is critical.

The venue

Restaurants are environments designed for pleasure. In fact, the first 'restaurants' (the word actually means a restorative soup), which appeared when chefs displaced from châteaux by the French Revolution started catering in Paris, were the very first time a third party had designed a consumable experience to be enjoyed by people he probably did not know. This artifice remains in restaurants today. A restaurant is a designed experience.

A pitch in an office is one thing; a pitch in a restaurant is still a pitch, but it is more informal, more relaxed, more indulgent and more diabolically subtle. A pitch is very often less a test of people's confidence in your idea and more a test of people's confidence in you. Hence the choice of restaurant is a clear indication of what you are like as a person. It betrays your knowledge, your tastes, your influence, your budget, your conversational skills, your entertainment potential and your savoir-faire. Subconsciously people want to deal with people they like and admire. Whether you are buying or selling, this is what is on test at lunch. Hence the acute sensitivities.

Any large city offers a meticulously graduated scale of restaurants whose profile may be appreciated and precisely adapted to the purposes of the pitch. Brillat-Savarin said, 'Tell me what you eat and I will tell you what you are.' This might today be adapted to read 'Tell me where you eat and I will tell you what you are trying to say.' There are no innocent choices in choosing a venue. Grimy old-school curry houses, pizza chains, gastropubs, unreformed Italians, modern Indian, *nuova cucina* Italians, unreformed French (now rare), advanced new French, Argentine, Belgian, brasseries, silly new British, impressive new British, grand hotels, hotels offering after-coffee fornication possibilities, Turkish, Greek, Thai, bistros, indeterminate Mediterranean, indeterminate Middle Eastern, kosher, Chinese, tapas, celebrity petting zoos with ambiguous cuisine, Basque, Korean, sushi, fusion, New York steakhouses, clubs (old), clubs (new), offal specialists . . . even Portuguese (but this is an extremely specialized option).

> **Tell me where you eat and I will tell you what you are trying to say.**

Every potential client or potential conquest has an ideal venue, perfectly suited in style and mood to the business in hand. Wherever it is, the maladroit will fret about getting the best table. Apart from being put near the kitchen and getting thwacked by the service doors on their bomber hinges, there really is no such thing. Finding myself on time for a late guest at a popular London celebrity petting zoo, I saw the next table was occupied by an influential magazine publisher. Short of something to do, I asked the hovering proprietor, 'If he's there and I'm here, I suppose that means I have the second-best table.' Masterfully, the reply quickly came: 'The best table is wherever *you* are sitting.'

The agenda

As in any pitch, lunch is an opportunity for information transfer, exchange of power and the chance to impress or even dominate. Equally, there is the chance to lose. Lunch is not a good place to present a structured argument, what with the intrusions of the wine waiter and the banal necessities of mastication and digestion, although the prudent person will have prepared a list of conversational topics which keep dialogue cheerfully afloat while steering it towards a desirable philosophical destination (usually involving the real or implied imminent increase in one party's wealth).

Crucial, of course, to decide at precisely what moment you make your play and ask the Big Question. This may be pitching for work or naming your price for a job already offered. There are cultural differences in the moment determined as ideal. Americans are often more open about the business purposes of lunch and make the proposition item number one on the agenda, thus occurring at the beginning of the meal. With the English, residual elements of gentlemanly squeamishness about the proletarian vileness of business remain and the Big Question is usually deferred until coffee. You can usually sense the deferral taking place. Each party knows something is going on and a tension exists between expectancy on one side and hesitancy on the other.

Menu deconstruction and the politesse of drinking

'Time spent in reconnaissance is seldom wasted' is a military principle that applies very well to the choice of restaurant. Unless there is merit in making lunch a pioneering voyage of gastronomic discovery (thus presenting yourself as a brave individualist, unafraid of novelty and rising above the rancid solemnities of popular opinion), best to choose the familiar. Little of advantage is gained by losing concentration and having to frown at an unfamiliar menu only to be told by a condescending waiter, 'I'm sorry, but the Tarabagani no sumibiyaki pirikana ponza gake is off.'

Instead, real advantage may be gained by genuine familiarity with the menu. First, all available concentration may be reserved for the performance instead of the interpretation and deconstruction of something perhaps designed to baffle and impress. Secondly, a pleasant worldliness is suggested by patiently acquired knowledge. 'I always have the fricassee of cods' tongues when here, but whether it's edible depends if Esteban is in the kitchen' is a line that conveys experience, knowledge and a pleasant tad of pained vulnerability. Equally, 'Don't touch the squid at this time of year, it's frozen and comes from Cambodia' suggests both impressive connoisseurship and a touching concern for a guest's palate, as well as a winning suggestion that the guest is sufficiently sophisticated to eschew

Lunch is not a good place to present a structured argument

deep refrigeration in favour of right-on seasonality. Mrs Thatcher always used to insist on anything skeletal being served off the bone or, if exo-skeletal, out of the shell, since to manoeuvre around such unnegotiable material might hinder conversation.

Then there is the exquisite choice to drink or not to drink. This is a question that involves many elaborate psychological bluffs and evasions. While no one would wish to enter that state which Tina Brown described as a 'sodden aria of indiscretion', it is gastronomically foolish to disdain a moderate amount of wine if eating appropriate food. (Norman Douglas used to say to Elizabeth David, 'Do you think we can manage a litre?' They could.) Equally, most hosts and guests, while having promised themselves very faithfully earlier that morning not to drink at lunch, would honestly admit to a soothing wave of relief to hear the other person say, 'Well, yes, maybe just a glass of white wine.' Besides, people who do not drink may, often correctly, be under suspicion of alcoholism.

People who do not drink may, often correctly, be under suspicion of alcoholism

As with the food menu, the wine list offers many opportunities to reveal a persuasively impressive knowledge of the subject. Equally, it presents many vicious traps for those who have economized on the time spent in reconnaissance. A good tip: never say the number of the wine since it suggests you cannot pronounce foreign languages. And then you are asked to make a judgement on your selection as a sample mouthful is presented as a taster. Great confidence is required to deal with sommeliers, and many people are justifiably harrowed by being asked to taste something they have in fact never tasted before, but the sommelier is not expecting a connossieur's opinion, only confirmation that a choice of wine is drinkable and permission to pour has been given.

Still, some may be tempted to score points with an informed comment. Stephen Potter suggested a policy of being 'boldly meaningless': say something ridiculous such as 'It's a little bit cornery' or 'Too many tramlines'. No one can argue. Or depart on pure fantasies, making guesses at supposed percentages of glucosity in different years. No one will challenge you. Or try, as Potter suggested, literary-based obfuscation: 'The sort of wine Miss Mitford's Emily would have offered Parson Square, sitting in the window seat behind the chintz curtains.' Me? I always ask for house wine. No decent restaurant would dare offer anything less than good. You appear confident, not parsimonious.

Loo breaks and other recovery stratagems

A great advantage of being familiar with a restaurant is that easy way you acquire of knowing about the loos. If arriving in a strange restaurant, best to reconnoitre the bathrooms before going to the table since few gestures in life and business look so pitiably gormless and destructive of confidence as helplessly floundering around, making false attacks at the service door, or having to ask disdainful waiters where you may go to seek relief. Sexual authority is not everything, but there is something emasculating about being too desperate to micturate. Besides, for maximum Machiavellian poise, a comfortable bladder is a necessity. And decent restaurants will also furnish the ambitious luncher with clothes brushes, mouthwash, hand cream and linen to polish up your shoes.

An old Foreign Office adage, offered to young diplomats, is

of special relevance to any guide about pitching over lunch. It maintained that you should never tell a lie, while avoiding telling the whole truth. And, more importantly, you should never miss an opportunity to go to the lavatory. This last not merely to make hydraulic adjustments to comfort, but possibly to send furtive texts, order a cab, tell your assistant to make calls so you sound busy, make notes or be absolutely certain you do not have an asparagus tip on the end of your nose.

> ❝ Be absolutely certain you do not have an asparagus tip on the end of your nose. ❞

In all matters, poise is essential. Very few people have won affection, respect or lucrative contracts by flapping. Panic is not our friend. For example, in one of his thirties travel books Evelyn Waugh described a diplomat who was sick on his plate during a formal lunch at an embassy. Without hesitation or drawing attention to himself (a true inheritor of Castiglione's philosophy of reserve), he continued to eat, unflustered. Recently a lunch guest had a nasty accident with an explosive croustade of quails' eggs with hollandaise, sending a spurt of bright yellow yolk across the table and on to my shirt. I like to think my conversation did not miss a beat. At all costs, however, avoid spilling wine since this unambiguously suggests you are drunk.

Sex

While most women know that 'Can I buy you dinner?' means 'Are you possibly available for sex afterwards?', at lunch the erotic dynamic is more subtle (although by no means insignificant). A woman may accept because she looks forward to the pleasure of saying yes. She may, perversely, accept because she looks forward to the pleasure of saying no. She may accept because she has not decided yet and is looking forward to sizing you up. To ask the dinner question of a woman is not so much to interrogate her as to offer yourself up for merciless interview and analysis.

In the dinner question, the woman has a choice. Having asked the question, the man has made his bid and is now the victim. But an invitation to lunch is an offer of a more ambiguous and enigmatic occasion. Dinner is sexual, while lunch may certainly be sexual, but is also social and possibly also commercial.

Truth is that if you pitch a business deal in a meeting, your audience knows what's happening and they are on their guard. If a man takes a woman out to dinner, she also knows what is happening and is also on her guard. But lunch is a more relaxed, disarming encounter. Lunch is when you can, along with your *costoletta di maiale*, eat your prey . . . when they are least expecting it.

SUMMARY

LUNCH

❑ Lunch is a pitch.

❑ If the luncher, choose venue carefully, reconnoitre loos.

❑ If lunchee, be prompt, but not early.

❑ Whoever you are, prepare an invisible agenda.

❑ If the luncher, know the menu and wine list.

❑ If the lunchee, select modest items.

❑ Remember, whatever is on the menu, the real business of lunch is information transfer.

7 How to be, er, confident, or, at least first, best or different

W AS THERE ever anybody more confident than Winston Churchill? With the shortcomings – moral, oratorical, practical, symbolic, aesthetic – of our present crop of international leaders very much in mind, it is interesting to reflect on that famous photograph of Britain's most revered warrior chieftain.

He stands pin-striped and pugnacious, bow-tied beneath a dark Homburg. He may have already enjoyed a glass or two of his favourite Pol Roger champagne (and it was his habit to start the day with a whisky and soda in bed: 'I have taken more out of alcohol than alcohol has taken out of me,' he once said). Clamped in his jaw is one of the eight to ten Romeo y Julieta cigars he smoked every day (a habit he picked up on furlough in Cuba in 1895, later maintaining a store of three thousand or so at his house in Kent). Additionally – a nice touch, this – he is holding a Thompson M1928 sub-machine gun. His gastronomy and good manners, his lack of snobbery, his wit, an eloquence inspired by Gibbon, the love of craft and his belief that painting makes you happy ... these were the substantial things that made Churchill great. But accessories helped

People who lack confidence are terrified of being wrong

to make the point that here is a confident national leader.

Other politicians and public figures have accessorized themselves to help establish an impressive persona. Gandhi wore austere clothing he had designed and knitted himself. General Patton liked to carry elaborately engraved and decorated pistols. Hollywood says he wore a pair, but he more generally wore only one, usually a Colt .45 revolver or a Smith & Wesson .357 Magnum. Folklore describes Patton's pistols (now in the Patton Museum of Cavalry and Armor, Fort Knox, Kentucky) as 'pearl-handled'. This used to infuriate the belligerent old

> **Only a pimp in a New Orleans whorehouse would carry a pearl-handled pistol**

warhorse, who roared, 'Only a pimp in a New Orleans whorehouse would carry a pearl-handled pistol.' Instead, Patton's pistols had ivory handles. But they made an emphatic point, nonetheless.

George W. Bush was, perhaps, made of less impressive stuff than Churchill, Gandhi or Patton, but was quick to learn the advantages of semantic positioning with the aid of props. Having become a boot-wearing Texan cowboy (he was actually born on the East Coast, at New Haven, Connecticut, home city of Yale University), the transformation was not sufficiently thoroughgoing to give a nation confidence in tongue-tied performances after the trauma of 9/11. Accordingly, immediately after the 2001 attacks, Bush's Director of Communications, Karen Hughes, rehearsed the President in rhetoric and his speechwriters in evocative economy so as to fashion something (apparently) heroically confident out of unpromising material. Significant and deliberate in this transformation was, when at Ground Zero, Bush's very visible use of an electronically amplified bullhorn, symbol of a newly charismatic leader. Entirely redundant, since broadcast media had made available all necessary technology for the Commander-in-Chief to communicate with a shocked nation, the bullhorn was the exact equivalent of Patton's pistols or Churchill's machine gun: a device that turned a hesitant and confused President into a dynamic, forceful and confident apparition of leadership.

Confidence may certainly be aided by meaningful accessories. When Flaubert's dippy clerks Bouvard and Pécuchet inherit their fortune they say: '*Nous ferons tout ce qui nous plaira! Nous laisserons pousser notre barbe!*' ('Now we can do whatever we want! We can grow beards!') For similar reasons many people choose a Tesla – but acquiring confidence is fundamentally a matter of will more than accessories. And it is, like so much in the area of self-identity, self-perpetuating. People who lack confidence are great votaries of the 'no' function in man: they are always ready with a reason why some suggested stratagem is impossible, difficult or merely just uncomfortable. There is always a reason not to do something because there is only one way of doing nothing, so it cannot be wrong. People who lack confidence are terrified of being wrong. By contrast, there is an infinity of different ways to do something, many of which will be erroneous. The confident person does not care.

Confident people are votaries of the 'yes' function: they can walk into parties, start a conversation, get a table. They only take yes for an answer. Occasionally aided by guns or bullhorns, a more subtle visual language also supports the confident individual. He moves at a certain speed; he holds people's stares; he is not neurotically animated, but practises evocative hand or face gestures with calm and precision; he does not mumble, but nor does he talk if it is unnecessary. Style may be the dress of thought; confidence is the style of economy. Confident people are not apologetic ... because they do not make mistakes. Or never appear to do so. If you want to see a confident person, look at Salvator Rosa's self-portrait in London's National Gallery. Swaggeringly handsome and self-possessed, the painter leans out of the picture over a slab with the inscription '*Aut tace aut loquere meliora silentio*'. ('Shut up, or say something useful.')

Confidence is highly infectious, maybe even contagious. Act confident and people will treat you with more respect, and this powers a virtuous circle of self-enhancement. Start with a little confidence and you end up with a lot. Everybody knows, after Disraeli, the confident person's motto: 'Never complain and never explain', but what is less well known is the rejoinder (which we owe to American writer Elbert Hubbard): 'Your friends do not need it and your enemies will not believe you anyway.' Confident people never make excuses. As the French say, '*Qui s'excuse, s'accuse.*' People who make excuses accuse themselves of a fundamental uncertainty. You are unlikely to win a pitch with serial professions of exculpation, or denials of responsibility. Or howls of dismay.

So who has got confidence and may we borrow some?

Psychologists know that there are exceptionally high incidences of low confidence among successful professional women (or, indeed, men in close touch with their feminine side). In 1949, before the liberating insights of early feminism, the anthropologist Margaret Mead, in her book *Male and Female*, argued that many women were fearful that 'success' would call into question their femininity and, therefore, took protective and evasive action, choosing humbling postures which preserved certain conventional gender expectations.

So who has got confidence and may we borrow some?

Women, she seemed to suggest, did not see confidence as an important survival characteristic.

This is one of the bases of what has become known as 'impostor syndrome', not a clinically recognized disorder, but evidently so widespread that it has become a commonplace topic in psychological discourse. The condition was identified by Pauline Clance and Suzanne Imes in a 1978 paper called 'The Impostor Phenomenon Among High-Achieving Women'. The symptoms of impostor syndrome are like a specification for the design of a low-confidence personality: sufferers feel phoney and anxious; they feel their success is transitory and undeserved; they live in dread of being discovered; they are eaten by self-doubt. Therapists nowadays offer a role-playing technique, suggesting sufferers act out the I-am-truly-successful-and-highly-intelligent role.

This is something that one truly successful and highly intelligent woman discovered by first principles many years before 1978. This was Beatrice Webb, founder of the London School of Economics, the person who coined the word 'consumerism'. Webb, despite her obvious intelligence and manifest achievements, was crippled by a lack of confidence. She explained to Bertrand Russell how she evolved a technique for dealing with it: 'If I ever felt inclined to be timid as I was going into a room full of people, I would say to myself, "You're the cleverest member of one of the cleverest families in the cleverest class of the cleverest nation in the world, why should you be frightened?"'

That is what might be called a confidence trick. Beatrice Webb's solution to the agonizing problems of self-doubt, a sort of systematic desensitization, had earlier been predicted and encouraged by Eleanor Roosevelt: 'You gain strength, courage, and confidence by every experience in which you really stop to look fear in the face . . . You must do the thing you think you cannot do.'

This may be like believing as many as six impossible things before breakfast, but the idea that we all have reserves of potential which might be released to make us more winning, persuasive, confident individuals was developed after the fantasies of Lewis Carroll into the Pragmatism of William James, who believed that: 'Compared to what we ought to be, we are only half awake. We are making use of only a small part of our physical and mental resources.' This conceit has its

> Trust yourself, You know more than you think you do.

equivalent in a nostrum of babycare pioneer Dr Benjamin Spock: 'Trust yourself. You know more than you think you do.'

The confident person trusts himself. Indeed, the confident person's relationship with himself goes beyond mere trust and into areas of absolute conviction about creative and intellectual superiority. But another underlying concept here is that people who lack confidence may be lazy and indulgent. They are reluctant to use all their resources, unwilling to be tested in difficult circumstances and, in a perverse way, comforted by failure. But being confident is just a matter of deciding to be confident. 'You gotta be first, best or different' was Loretta Lynn's advice. 'You've got to take risks' was General MacArthur's. He said, 'There is no security on this earth, there is only opportunity.' The confident person finds insecurity stimulating and opportunity exciting.

Perhaps the very deepest principle in human nature is to be admired. This is the condition the confident person enjoys. Citing Plato's thymos, American commentator David Brooks wrote of George W. Bush that he 'is a thymotic man partially chastened by Christianity'. This may be a poor example, but it explains the need for admiration in a certain personality type. Brooks also explained that when workers have the confidence to go on strike, what is at stake is respect and recognition, not a few percentage points. Self-worth is what replaces self-doubt in the confident person.

Confident people have a sort of authority that sociologist Max Weber, using a New Testament Greek word meaning 'state of grace', described as 'charisma', or what is more vernacularly known as 'presence', that attention-getting gravitas some people possess. These are the types who change the dynamic of a room, who create their own emotional weather system. Narcissism (helpfully defined by the American Psychiatric Association's *Diagnostic and Statistical Manual* as 'a pervasive pattern of grandiosity, need for admiration and lack of empathy') is one way of describing the confidence trick.

But Weber's charisma is more mysterious and noble; he even claimed it might have a divine origin. He says the charismatic person is 'set apart from ordinary men and treated as endowed with supernatural, superhuman, or at least specifically exceptional powers or qualities' quite beyond the access of ordinary people. Charisma means brimful of confidence, the ability to win the assent of any audience. Or to win a pitch.

SUMMARY

HOW TO BE, ER, CONFIDENT

- ❏ Confidence is self-perpetuating. Create some and you will soon have more.
- ❏ Make yourself do what you fear.
- ❏ Remember: you know more than you think you do.
- ❏ Be first, best or different.

8 The importance of malice, or, bad behaviour and good results

'WITH RESPECT . . .' As soon as you hear those words it's clear the speaker intends not to be respectful, but scornful, insolent, critical, abusive and possibly even . . . malicious. Equally, when someone says 'But joking apart' it is – as Hugh Kingsmill explained in his classic anthology of *Invective and Abuse* (1929), an exhilarating catalogue of malicious commentary across the ages – usually the first time the audience realizes the speaker had had any mirthful intent in the first place.

Being disliked can be a powerful stimulus to enhanced performance.

It's at this moment the speaker has a plan to make his point, to pitch his idea. And the purpose of this chapter is to say that there are occasions when malice, or at least an element of *rudeness*, truculence or obstreperousness can help. Being disliked can be a powerful stimulus to enhanced performance. Making a case for malicious and abusive behaviour may, at first, seem cynical and barbaric. Instead, think of it as sophisticated and cultivated, a mark of intellectual superiority. As Sigmund Freud knew: 'The man who first flung a word of abuse at his enemy instead of a spear was the founder of civilization.'

You cannot win souls in an empty church, and by the same logic you are unlikely to make your point effectively if no one is listening to you. An intelligent, economical measure of (mild-mannered and good-natured) malice can help fill the pews for your sermon. Abraham Lincoln believed that if you want to make the most of yourself, avoid contention, but on this occasion he was wrong. Being contentious is a very good way of drawing attention to yourself and then to your proposition. And unless you have someone's attention, you cannot possibly win their hearts or minds . . . or their business.

The meek do not inherit the fast lane

I have mixed feelings about goodness. It's marvellous that the poet Jean Lorrain, who fought a duel with Marcel Proust in 1897 and was described by Philippe Julian as Sodom's Ambassador to Paris (*un erotomane, travesti, homme de grand vice*) thought 'a bad reputation never did anyone any harm'. He would know: he had one. Sex, drink and drugs were his currency.

It is really quite hard to prove that unblemished virtue is an asset to a business, or, indeed, to any sort of relationship. Indeed, it is easy to make the opposite case. Perhaps not all the seven deadly sins are useful in management and romance: sloth, for example, is no-one's friend, but avarice and lust are terrific motivators.

Meanwhile, no-one is going to publish a book called *Seven Saintly Stratagems to Protect Your Bottom Line* because it would be very boring and would not sell, but *Unscrupulous Advice from the Very Rich* would surely be an attractive title, and a thicker volume.

Hunter S. Thompson once said, looking around his friends and colleagues and, indeed, looking at himself, that considering how very happy and successful everyone was, he would positively recommend committed, long-term abuse of drugs and alcohol. It is the same with sin. We may need more of it.

I am not talking about vulgar criminals, although common criminals and business visionaries share certain traits: they both have huge egos and see a system that is vulnerable to exploitation for personal gain. Of course, criminality is not in itself attractive, although its disguises may be. Remember that the Ponzi scheme fraudster Bernard Madoff had many admirers and investors until the very end. Like the German intellectuals with the Nazis, a great many otherwise sensible people found Madoff entirely plausible.

Instead, there is a more subtle case to be made for the place of wickedness. And this case has historical credentials so profound that it is tempting to argue a general theory that business and romantic life are amoral and that a record of social conscience or good behaviour or polite deference or well-maintained scruples or good time-keeping or fidelity do not necessarily make any contribution to success. They might even militate against it. We know this. William Randolph Hearst was the US newspaper magnate who invented popular journalism, made himself one of the world's richest men in the process, and inspired the classic movie *Citizen Kane*. But I doubt that you'd have heard any of his contemporaries saying 'William, what a lovely fellow.'

Any survey of sin's place in culture must begin with Cesare Borgia, the illegitimate son of a Pope and one of the great soldiers, statesmen, murderers and corrupters of the Renaissance era. Borgia existed in a stew of universal depravity where incest, back-stabbing, front-stabbing and poisoning were routine. He was the inspiration for Niccolo Machiavelli's *The Prince*. This was the first how-to book, just as Machiavelli was the prototype management consultant. His top tip was that the ends justify the means. Decide what you want and go for it.

Theft is a common theme in success. The men whose iron, coal and railroads made industrial America possible were called 'Robber Barons', not 'Civic-Minded Philanthropists'. The Japanese camera industry, now recognized as the world leader, started life with cheap copies of more costly European originals. Picasso too knew that truly great artists don't borrow, they steal. Between inspiration and theft there is a line so fine it is nearly invisible.

Henry Ford used armed thugs to break strikes and was a virulent anti-Semite. During the Second World War, Mercedes-Benz and BMW 'employed' slave labour to manufacture war material. Ferdinand Porsche mumbled he was 'just doing his job' when he put his design consultancy in the service of Hitler, creating Panzer tanks and supervising manufacture of the V-1 buzz bomb. The war encouraged business duplicity: after 1945, the old US ITT conglomerate claimed compensation for damage caused by Allied bombing of the Focke-Wulf factories it owned. Good business, but questionable scruples.

In more recent times, suspicion that Coca-Cola subverts governments and certainties that it sells destructive, obesity-inducing products have not stopped it becoming the world's biggest beverage business. Steve Jobs was borderline psychotic, a bully and had sub-optimal personal hygiene. Bernie Ecclestone has only recently begun to talk openly about his long-alleged involvement with the Great Train Robbery. He denied it all, adding, mischievously, that there was not, in any case, enough money on the train to make the heist worthwhile in strict business terms.

High achievement does not necessarily equate to high principles. A friend of mine once went to a meeting with a leading retailer. She was a case-hardened PR Executive and quite inured to deplorable manners, but returned astonished that he had spent the entirety of her pitch talking on his phone, then passed wind very loudly, gave her a bottle of claret, patted her on the bottom and bade her farewell. This man was a titan of commerce, a vast SUV in the tiny car park of British business.

The question is not so much about sin, but the more general reality that many of life's activities discourage morality and encourage loutishness. For example, to make progress in traffic, good manners and foresight are actual handicaps. Traffic rewards brutality and stupidity. The meek do not inherit the fast lane.

Still, we admire success, even if we are often unhappy about the way it has been achieved. The moral mutability is revealed in that marvellous line of Malcolm McLaren's about his technically inept fledgling band, The Sex Pistols: 'They are so bad, they are good'. There's a thought.

A conversation is a variety of pitch: charm, intelligence, greed, knowledge, deception, opportunism, self-advancement and erotic suggestion all have their parts to play in effective and amusing dialogue, but so too does being rude. Not as a constant, unwavering attack, but – like the sharp capers that lift bland mayonnaise to piquant sauce tartare – as an ingredient to lift any conversation or presentation above and out of the ordinary. Be light, stinging, insolent and melancholy was drama critic Kenneth Tynan's communications dictum posted on his desk to keep him alert. It is certain to get you noticed. There is sometimes a price to be paid for being stinging and insolent, but Voltaire decided '*Mieux perdre un ami, qu'un bon mot.*' You can imagine the expression on his face when he said this: as Victor Hugo once remarked, Jesus wept while Voltaire smiled. It may be debatable whether it is more damaging to risk losing a friend than to miss the opportunity to be witty, but what is certain is that well-judged malice demands a response and engagement. And with engagement, you can make your pitch.

Chapter XVII of Machiavelli's *Prince* is titled 'Cruelty and Compassion; and whether it is better to be Loved than Feared, or the Reverse'. Of course, Machiavelli's moral neutrality (some would say his moral nihilism) allowed any course of action that got the desired results. His feeling was that to win a pitch, any slavish concern with the popular conception of what comprised 'good' manners or 'good' behaviour was not, shall we say, *necessary*. Be compassionate if you must, but do not neglect the possible winning effects of cruelty, was his advice. It is pleasant to be loved and admired, but being feared has its advantages too. Hence the importance of an element of

Usually qualified by the adjective 'cheap', abuse can be a very valuable tool.

controlled malice in human affairs. It was once said of the fierce putty-faced basilisk Sir John Pope-Hennessy, director of London's Victoria & Albert Museum, then of New York's Metropolitan Museum, that it was astonishing someone could rise to the very top of their profession by being so consistently disagreeable. Others might argue it was more predictable than astonishing.

So what is the process? The lowest order of malicious discourse is irony, a figure of speech in which the intended meaning is the opposite to the one conveyed by the words themselves. Czeslaw Milosz called irony 'the glory of slaves' and there are many problems in its application, not least that if your audience lacks the sophisticated device of ironic detachment then what you say will be interpreted at face value. Which is to say you will be completely misunderstood. There is less ambiguity in invective. Irony becomes invective, an educated insult, when detachment is deliberately abandoned in favour of *attack*. The process continues. Invective then evolves, or deteriorates, depending how Machiavellian you feel, into abuse. Usually qualified by the adjective 'cheap', abuse can be a very valuable tool. The current legal definition of aggravated damages is helpful here. Aggravated damages may be caused by 'malevolence, spite, malice, insolence and arrogance, intended to humiliate, distress or cause pain'.

Machiavelli would certainly advocate the use of humiliation, distress and pain, anything in fact to win a pitch, but history offers many other stimulating champions of abusive discourse. Martin Luther said Henry VIII was 'a pig, an ass, a dunghill, the spawn of an adder, a basilisk, a lying buffoon, a mad fool with a frothy mouth . . . a lubberly ass'. John Knox took on women. He wrote his 'First Blast of the Trumpet Against the Monstrous Regiment of Women' in Dieppe and it was published in Geneva in 1558. Designed perhaps to speed the imminent demise of Mary Tudor, it shows Knox unafraid of causing offence. Indeed, his 'Blast' was construed by the future Queen Elizabeth as a malicious insult. 'To promote a Woman to beare rule, superioritie, dominion, or empire above any Realme, Nation, or Citie, is repugnant to Nature; contumelie to God, a thing most contrarious to His reveled will and approved ordinance; and finallie, it is the subversion of good Order, of all equitie and justice . . .'

The exchange between John Wilkes, the political adventurer, and the Earl of Sandwich in 1763 was a malicious classic: a simple robust insult being magnificently trumped by wit of genius. 'Wilkes,' said Sandwich in orotund aristocratic tones, 'I don't know whether you'll die upon the gallows or of the pox.' Wilkes replied, 'That depends, my lord, whether I first embrace your lordship's principles, or your lordship's mistress.'

> **❝ I don't know whether you'll die upon the gallows or of the pox.' Wilkes replied, 'That depends, my lord, whether I first embrace your lordship's principles, or your lordship's mistress. ❞**

Another example. In what he hilariously (and ironically) described as 'language of the strictest reserve', Algernon Charles Swinburne wrote in 1874 a revenging letter to the American poet Ralph Waldo Emerson, whose appearance, character and disposition he described thus: 'A gap-toothed and hoary-headed ape, carried at first into notice on the shoulder of Carlyle, and who now in his dotage spits and chatters from a dirtier perch of his own finding and fouling: coryphaeus or choragus of his Bulgarian tribe of auto-coprophragous baboons, who make the filth they feed on . . .'

Or the critic Ruskin on the painter Whistler in 1877 in a dispute about the nature, value and cost of art. Ruskin, outraged at Whistler's opportunistic pricing policies: '. . . the ill-educated conceit of the artist so nearly approached the aspect of wilful imposture. I have seen, and heard, much of cockney impudence before now; but never expected to hear a coxcomb ask two hundred guineas for flinging a pot of paint in the public's face.' The following year Whistler replied: 'A life passed among pictures makes not a painter . . . As well allege that he who lives in a library must needs die a poet.'

More recently malicious comment has flourished in American literature. The novelist Truman Capote said that Jack Kerouac was not a writer, but a typist. Of Madeleine Albright as Secretary of State, Gore Vidal said: 'The typing pool's loss has not been diplomacy's gain.' John Updike, in a debate about the Great American Novel, said of Tom Wolfe, author of the best-selling *Bonfire of the Vanities*, that he was a mere illustrator who 'gropes and struggles for focus' and, in a masterstroke of malicious literary snobbery, added that Wolfe wrote 'entertainment, not literature'. The New York literary establishment takes pleasure in baiting the bestselling and swaggering Wolfe. John Irving said of Wolfe's *A Man in Full*, the successor to *Bonfire*, that it was 'like reading a bad newspaper or a bad piece in a magazine. It makes you wince.' The author of *The World According*

> The lead dog is the one they always try to bite in the ass.

to Garp said that on any page of Wolfe he could find a sentence that would make him gag. Wolfe shot back 'insular, effete and irrelevant'; he then called Irving's peers Norman Mailer and Updike 'two old piles of bones'.

Then Norman Mailer himself joined in. Reading *A Man in Full,* he said, was like making love to a 300-lb woman: 'Once she gets on top, it's all over. Fall in love or get asphyxiated.' Mailer also said that to his mind there was something silly about a man who went around New York in a white suit. Wolfe said Mailer and his cronies, who had had between them neither a *succès de scandale* nor a *succès d'estime* in years, were frightened and panicked by his success. 'The lead dog is the one they always try to bite in the ass,' Wolfe said. Mailer rejoined, 'It doesn't mean you're the top dog just because your ass is bleeding.' Politeness would not have got this literary debate recorded.

> **It doesn't mean you're the top dog just because your ass is bleeding.**

Since Whistler and Ruskin there have been many bravura malicious exchanges between artist and critic. Robert Hughes said sculptor Jeff Koons 'couldn't carve his name on a tree' and, despairing of his subject, said accusing a crass self-publicist such as Koons 'of hype is like rebuking a fish for being wet', adding that he possessed 'a vulgarity so syrupy, gross and numbing that collectors felt challenged by it'. The novelist William Boyd nicely described all late-twentieth-century art as 'a wet fart of faddery, flim-flam and self indulgence'.

A malicious comment is designed to be confrontational, to disarm. It is therefore the conversational equivalent of military psy-ops, the psychological operations which the army nicely describes as a non-lethal weapons system. An assumption of psy-ops, as in malicious discourse, is that you need first to understand the enemy's or the client's motivations and vulnerabilities. Use of logic and stimulation of fear and desire are the tools. To compromise self-belief is the aim. Indeed, US specialists insist that it is more important to target the opponent's beliefs than to express your own. For instance, US Army propaganda always shows bananas in bowls of fruit being offered to surrendering Iraqis since from Basra to Baghdad the banana is prized as a special delicacy with extraordinary allure and bewitching associations of luxury and excess. The banana is, at least in this context, a stimulus of desire.

The classical world offers an early example of the psy-ops principle of stimulating fear: Alexander the Great left behind carefully fabricated dramatically oversized armour to cause consternation in the passing enemy. Psy-ops, if successful, vitiates the need for combat. In China Sun Tzu argued that the very last thing you want to do is actually attack a person or a city. You're much more likely get a result by undermining not walls, but the enemy's strategy. In the Second World War the British persuaded the Germans that technology was in place to set fire to the Channel and psychologically disarming radio broadcasts told listeners (in perfect German) how to say: 'I am burning', 'The water is very cold' and 'The boat is sinking'. Less successfully, 'Baghdad Betty' broadcast to US troops that their wives were all sleeping with the cartoon character Bart Simpson. Here, faulty research undermined a psy-ops campaign. But the principle was sound: all psy-ops and all malicious discourse, invective and abuse depend for their effect on . . . emotion.

Although the Iraqis found the invocation of Bart Simpson as a predatory stud unhelpful in generating sexual jealousy and concomitant low morale amongst American troops, the erotic is a rich mine to be plundered for emotional weapons. Marcel Proust recommended calculated insults based on this principle. His psy-ops advice to women

The facts given may be arranged in any convenient order.

was that negative behaviour can often yield positive results. An absence, an invitation refused, a certain coldness, separately, or combined, could accomplish more than cosmetics or costume. This works the other way too. Sexually shocking bluntness rarely goes unnoticed and can have dramatic effects. Virginia Woolf recalled the moment of her psychological liberation when all barriers of reticence were for ever after broken down. It was 1908 and Lytton Strachey looked at a stain on the skirt of her sister, Vanessa Bell, and asked 'Semen?'

Pure disinformation, intended to demoralize, confuse or disturb, is another effectively malicious tool in argument. H. E. Dale's *The Higher Civil Service of Great Britain* (1941) has often been cited as the classical source of a non-lethal disinformation system. His advice to politicians is a masterclass in cynicism. It now reads as comedic, but was written with the serene pomp of an undisturbed mandarin:

> Nothing may be said which is not true; but it is as unnecessary as it is sometimes undesirable, even in

the public interest, to say everything relevant which is true; and the facts given may be arranged in any convenient order. It is wonderful what can be done within these limits by a skilful draughtsman. It might be said, cynically, but with some measure of truth, that the perfect reply to an embarrassing question in the House of Commons is one that is brief, appears to answer the question completely, if challenged can be proved to be accurate in every word, gives no opening for awkward 'supplementaries', and discloses really nothing.

In the same way that small doses of arsenic may be stimulating, malice is useful in life. Not the 'gleeful spiritual aggression' which Erving Goffman attributed to the con man, nor the systematic belligerence of the uncultivated boor, but something more calculated: 'A slight touch of friendly malice and amusement towards those we love keeps our affection for them from turning flat', according to American Bloomsburyite Logan Pearsall Smith. A slight touch of malice is even more useful in business since it demands a level of response and engagement that is the prologue to a pitch.

Of course, even the judicious use of malice can have damaging side effects. People may dislike – even hate – you. But hatred has a special quality of its own. Lord Byron knew its paradoxical nature. In Don Juan there is a couplet:

Now hatred is by far the longest pleasure;
Men love in haste, but they detest at leisure.

The same idea was taken up by Benjamin Robert Haydon, a friend of Keats and Wordsworth, in his pamphlet 'On Hating', in which he argued that hate is preferable to love because it lasts longer. And what is politics itself but the systematic organization of hatreds?

Anyway, Machiavelli would argue that being hated for being malicious does not matter provided people do what you want. With respect, bad can be useful and enjoyable.

SUMMARY

THE IMPORTANCE OF MALICE

❏ Negative behaviour can get positive results.

❏ Being disarming demands attention.

❏ Compromise the target's self-belief.

❏ A little malice keeps relationships fresh.

9 Where do ideas come from?

CREATIVE THINKING, Maurice Saatchi once said, is the last legal way to secure an unfair advantage. It is an essential element in any pitch.

But what exactly is creative thinking? Where do ideas come from? Some people have lots. Many have none at all. You need lots of ideas to be creative, because in an area bereft of certainties one thing is quite clear: creativity is inspired by ideas and information. The more you have, the better off you are. And creativity can be defined as the capacity to put ideas and information together in unprecedented, unusual, unpredictable ways.

Porsche's chief designer once explained that his inspiration came from: modern sculpture; animal morphology; the zonked-out anaerobic state brought

Stanley Spencer found his muse by sticking his head in a lavatory bowl.

about during a strenuous run; ski boots; the Hong Kong Peak Ferry; escalators; the smell of new cars; and Pat Metheny's jazz-rock album *As Falls Wichita, So Falls Wichita Falls*. By way of contrast, the painter Stanley Spencer found his muse by sticking his head in a lavatory bowl. William James felt that alcohol, being a votary of the 'yes' function in man, was a valuable creative tool.

Most people believe they are thinking when they are really only rearranging their prejudices. There is some scientific evidence to suggest that our capacity for information-processing is inherently modest. Humans have low bandwidth, or so it was suggested by George A. Miller in a well-known 1956 *Psychological Review* article entitled 'The Magical Number Seven, Plus or Minus Two: Some Limits on Our Capacity for Processing Information'. Miller said we can only handle seven pieces of information at a time. But maybe learning to handle more would be an advantage. We have to learn to do this and, at the same time, to be receptive to novelty. Life may be lived forwards, but only understood backwards. This is why creativity is so unpredictable and hard to define: it only ever goes forwards.

History has wonderful examples of individuals lacking the creative intelligence to take a bet on the future. Banker J. Pierpont Morgan told Alexander Graham Bell, 'My colleague and I have seen and discussed your invention, but we have determined there is no commercial future for it.' He was, of course, speaking of the telephone. In 1945 officials from the British Intelligence Objectives Sub-Committee, using consultants from the now forgotten Humber Car Company, took one look at a factory in Wolfsburg and said its chief product was 'not to be regarded as an example of first-class modern design to be copied by British industry'. They spoke of the ineffable Volkswagen. At the same time, ICI rejected Agfa's colour film technology as 'commercially uninteresting', whereupon the scientists involved went to Rochester, New York, to visit Kodak, where they discovered a different point of view. Because Stafford Cripps's Christian Socialist principles made the British reluctant to 'profit' from German defeat, the engineers who developed swept-wing technology and trans-sonic flight all themselves flew to Boeing or America's National Advisory Council on Aeronautics.

Timidity is rarely, if ever, a characteristic of creative thinking. Nor is conservatism in dress or thought or appetite: there are hundreds of thousands of edible plants on the planet, but we eat only about six hundred of them. Nor too is consistency (a commodity dismissed by Lord Acton as a 'puerile temptation'). Like many creative people Albert Einstein was illogical and contradictory (not to mention untidy). Explaining his discovery (or perhaps it was his 'invention') of the principle of relativity he said: 'I simply *ignored* an axiom.'

Nothing defines creativity better than the ability to defeat habit by originality. This originality seems to come from people best able to exploit the potential of a brain containing ten billion cells, each one capable of making about five thousand connections. The quest for novelty was brilliantly described by jazz musician Miles Davis when he said, 'Don't play what's there. Play what's not there.' This invocation of the creative negative was also used by Akio Morita, who said his Sony company's philosophy was 'doing what others did not'. In Morita's case, his greatest creative act was to realize that Western Electric's semiconductor (which its inventors William Shockley, John Bardeen and Walter Brattan had considered useful only as a device for making scientific measurements in laboratories) might most profitably be used in transistor radios. His second most creative act was to realize that 'Sony' (which creatively conflates the Latin root for sound with the affectionate, if misspelt, name for a male child) worked better than the original name Tokyo Tsushin Kogyo Kabushika Kaisha.

> **Don't play what's there. Play what's not there.**

Creative thinking depends on absurdity and the nerve to embrace failure. One of the chief principles of the New Absurdity was defined by a 3M scientist who was responsible for the Post-it note: looking for a powerful adhesive, he only managed to concoct a weak one . . . but with the virtue of re-use which created a new category of office product. He said of his impressive failure, 'If I knew what I was doing, it wouldn't be research.'

And nor does the New Absurdity need to be moral. Picasso was only the best-known individual to claim that great artists don't borrow, they steal. This is what you might call the importance of unfair-dealing. Unreasonableness also plays its part: Picasso said, 'I am always doing that which I cannot do, in order that I may learn how to do it.' Ludwig Wittgenstein believed: 'If people never did silly things, nothing intelligent would get done.' And nor does the creative thinker of the New Absurdist school respect the rancid orthodoxies of accounting. The film director Billy Wilder once said 'There's one thing you never hear and it's this: "Gee ! I must go and see that movie! I hear it came in under budget."'

Although 'Brainstorming' is often advocated as a stimulus, it is rarely effective since it's a bureaucratic concept rather than a creative one. Creative thinkers tend to be exploitative and solitary, neither team players nor attractive social models. Brainstorming was invented by adman Alex Osborn in his 1950s business bestseller *Applied Imagination*. He neglected the fact that creativity is individual, not communal. Indeed, one test for creativity is that sharing with the group is rejected and constructive criticism not tolerated. Beethoven was not a brainstormer and once told some violinists grumbling over a difficult passage to shut up and get on with it because he didn't care what they thought and, in any case, God had helped him write it. Bob Dylan, when he first played electric at the 1965 Newport Folk Festival, told a jeering audience, 'I follow no one.' As a management tool, Brainstorming can take its place in the graveyard of uncreative ideas that includes Downsizing, Outsourcing, Benchmarking, Total Quality Management, Management by Objectives and Business Process Re-engineering. Crowd-sourcing has not yet created a hit song.

But if it is impossible to manage the process of creative thinking in an orderly manner, there have been some remarkable attempts to evaluate the quality of its results. In 1948 Claude Shannon published a paper titled 'A Mathematical Theory of Communication' in the *Bell System Technical Journal*. The very invention that Pierpont Morgan said had no future had by mid-century created one of the world's leading research laboratories. Shannon was a remarkable creative figure. Although his technical expertise was in the, perhaps to some arid, areas of relay switches and cleaning-up the acoustics of phone lines, he had a creative intelligence which helped him see the larger picture and a brain that worked like a busy telephone exchange, constantly making connections.

> **Beethoven was not a brainstormer and once told some violinists grumbling over a difficult passage to shut up and get on with it because he didn't care what they thought and, in any case, God had helped him write it.**

He adapted the word 'entropy' from thermodynamics and in giving it a metaphysical character added a new idea to thought on human behaviour. He made the distinction between signal and noise and distinguished between mere data (measurements) and the more valuable information (data which has a value that affects behaviour). The binary mathematics that moved civilization from the analog to the digital age was Shannon's invention and he made the distinction between medium and message, influencing Marshall McLuhan. This last technical distinction between form and content allowed engineers to concentrate on technology, freeing the rest of us. In a single paper Shannon established the principles of Information Theory and predicted the convergence of phones and computers. If the digital age had a father, if the information culture had a founder, it was Claude Shannon. And he did all of this without any respect for what had gone before. Shannon said, 'I had to *invent* any maths that was needed.'

Audacity, not to say fearlessness, is another characteristic of the creative individual. Being right is not necessarily the issue. And nor is dim consensus. Shannon's successor at Bell Labs, a Nobel laureate, once explained that in a business culture if everybody thinks it's a good idea, then – whatever it is – it probably isn't. So a tolerance for mistakes is another creative characteristic.

Henry Ford described failure as a blessing, an 'opportunity to begin again more intelligently'.

James Joyce called mistakes the 'portals of discovery'. Thomas Watson, founder of IBM, said, 'If you want to succeed, double your failure rate.' Soichiro Honda believed that 'success represents the one per cent of your work that results from the 99 per cent that's called failure'. Henry Ford described failure as a blessing, an 'opportunity to begin again more intelligently'.

Unfortunately for the good administration of business, the creative personality is definitively at odds with business disciplines. This is recognized in the well-established concept of triarchic intelligence. First, the analytical intelligence of the mathematician. Second, the practical intelligence of the architect. Third, the creative intelligence of, shall we say, Johannes Brahms, who explained that when he had a new musical idea he would leave it alone for a while and then, when he returned to it, the idea would have developed all by itself. Thackeray found his own creative processes bewildering. When he had written something amusing, he asked himself, 'How did I think of that?'

To be creative you have to establish unusual hierarchies. Significantly, creative processes are entirely at odds with the core ideas of teaching: authority, explanation, reasoning and evidence. Instead, creativity seems to an extent to be based on (possible) alcohol abuse, theft, solitariness, tolerance of mistakes, deliberate misunderstandings and dissent.

The creative intelligence refuses convention. When asked what he was going to play, Miles Davis said, 'I'll play it first and tell you what it is later.'

I'll play it first and tell you what it is later

But there may be a partial answer to the question 'Where do ideas come from?' Memory. For the ancient Greeks, memory was the province of the gods. The mother of the nine Muses was called Mnemosyne (from the Greek for 'remembrance').

Knowledge is a function of memory and, since creativity is a function of knowledge, training the memory may be the most straightforward way to enjoy the possibility of sharing in Maurice Saatchi's unfair advantage.

Memory became a part of rhetoric and devices for training memory became known as mnemonics. Significantly, it was discovered that an efficient method of training memory was for the orator to imagine a complex building with warrens of interconnected rooms. In every room the orator would place ideas and when it was necessary to remember them, he would simply revisit the imaginary building, literally recollecting ideas as his imagination wandered down the corridors, ante-rooms and chambers of a fantastical architectural plan. This old tradition of a 'memory palace' surfaced in England in a 1562 translation by William Fulwood called *The Castle of Memorie*, although its most celebrated exponent was an Italian Jesuit called Matteo Ricci. In 1577 Ricci set out for China, where he wrote a book on the art of memory in Chinese, a title which became popular with Ming dynasty opinion-formers. The architectural metaphors of memory survive in the technobabble of computer jargon.

When trained, the brain can achieve astonishing technical feats of recall. The seventeenth-century English mathematician John Wallis could compute a fifty-three-digit square root in his head. When the novelist Samuel Butler wanted to make a new edition of Shakespeare's *Sonnets*, he felt he could not possibly do so without memorizing them all word-perfect. This he did in a year when he was also writing two novels. John von Neumann, the games theoretician and computer pioneer who coined the term 'bit', could memorize whole books verbatim.

But there is an artistic side to memory as well. What the psychologists call the 'cued retrieval of explicit memory, characterized by episodic content where the spatial component of the context is particularly important', provides one of the great moments in literature. With some unsalted butter, an egg, vanilla essence, caster sugar, sifted flour and grated orange peel you can make a cake known as a madeleine. When Marcel Proust ate one in conjunction with a tisane of lime blossom, he experienced an explosion of memory and was prompted to go in search of '*l'édifice immense du souvenir*' (another architectural metaphor).

Alcohol, plans of buildings, the taste of cakes. All these can stimulate the unusual connections that are the basis of creative thinking. But you can also win an unfair advantage just by accumulating more ideas and information than the next man.

SUMMARY

WHERE DO IDEAS COME FROM?

❑ Creativity depends on access to ideas and information.

❑ Rearranging prejudices is not the same as thinking.

❑ Be unusual, be arbitrary and be prepared to accept mistakes.

❑ Defeat habits.

❑ Memory should be exercised like a muscle.

10 Visual language, or, what does my tattoo say about me?

ACCORDING TO Machiavelli: 'The great majority of mankind is satisfied with appearances.' Mrs Thatcher's reputation manager, Tim Bell, had the same conceit five centuries later when he insisted that 'perceptions are real'. Successful cosmetic surgeon Laurence A. Kirwan says, 'Changing your appearance can dramatically change your life.' Looks matter. Dr Kirwan's stirring business credo is: look like a slob, feel like a slob. But how exactly do we interpret the appearances of people and things? Perceptions may, indeed, be real, but how do we make sure others have a favourable perception of us? It may not be a true impression, but so long as it's a favourable one, that's an advantage. That's the nature of a successful pitch.

The science of non-verbal communications is concerned with how facial expressions, eye contact, postures, gestures, personal space and paralinguistics can be read. This last is specially interesting. Paralinguistics is the non-verbal aspects of speech: the use of pauses and punctuation, the silent semi-colon, the ability to be apparently speaking in capitals or, as London's most flamboyant literary agent was once described, 'being fluent in his second language: italics',

> **The great majority of mankind is satisfied with appearances.**

this to suggest an inclination towards irony. But apart from speaking in italics, there is a whole catalogue of behaviour that can determine a favourable response from lovers, friends, audiences and clients. Those with an inclination to brag or exaggerate should know that Frederick the Great's advice to his troops was: 'Be more than you seem.' Keep those appearances understated.

One of the pioneers of non-verbal communication was Ray L. Birdwhistell (1918–1994), a ballet dancer turned anthropologist, latterly holding a chair in the Annenberg School for Communications in the University of Pennsylvania. Birdwhistell established the study of kinesics, a 'kine' being the smallest measurable unit (or quantum) of a body movement. To study the way we move in space and how, consciously or unconsciously, we establish meaning by arranging our eyes and body parts in certain patterns, Birdwhistell made an eighty-minute black and white 16-mm film, known as TRD 009, located in the bar of a London hotel.

The focus was how listeners responded to speakers. A raised eyebrow here. Leaning in to listen closely and establish intimacy there. The steepling of the hands to convey thoughtfulness (later comprehensively described by G. I. Nierenberg and H. H. Calero in *How to Read a Person like a Book* (1973)). Leaning back in mock amazement. Wrinkling the nose (using the *levator labii superioris alaquae nasi* muscles). Touching the elbow of your communicant to import earnestness. Or had it been in an Italian bar, the rocking of a down-turned hand to say 'I'm not so very sure' about any given proposition.

The first Italian book on hand gestures was published by Andrea Jorio in Naples in 1832, with nineteen illustrations. The idea was taken up by Milanese designer Bruno Munari in his *Supplemento al Dizionario Italiano* (1963), a photo-guide to hand gestures, mentioned here earlier, whose value and entertainment is slightly diminished by his disappointing reluctance to include 'the vulgar ones', including the mandatory grabbing of the testicles to avert the evil eye.

The most well known and unambiguous hand gesture is the Great British V-sign, just a little less gross – because more compact – than the Continental forearm jerk, although no less reliably insulting. Widely assumed to be ancient and unambiguously interpreted as a manual equivalent to the labio-dental fricative (which is to say the shape the mouth forms when saying 'fuck off'), its origins are debated. No photograph of a V-sign earlier than 1913 is known (and this was taken, one is tempted to write 'inevitably', at a football match), although folklore maintains the obscene insult came from Agincourt, where English archers mocked French opponents with the two fingers that were to power their defeat by bows and arrows. There is a reference to a derisive V-sign in Rabelais, although the most scholarly explanation is that the V-sign evolved from the Roman digitus impudicus, the phallic mid-finger which the abusively inclined still find effective non-verbal communication today.

Personal Space is scientifically defined as a zone around your body from 0.5 metre to 1.2 metres.

These are only a few examples from an available infinity of

gestures which communicate at least as powerfully as words. Personal space, or proxemics, is another part of the territory of non-verbal communication. Here a clear hierarchy was established by Edward Hall in his book *The Silent Language* (1959). Basically, the precise distance you stand from someone is a way of immediately establishing the character of your relationship long before you say 'I love you' or 'Do I know you?' There are four generally agreed types of proximity: Public Space, when you are at least 3 metres away from another person. In this zone, personal communication is impossible, although long-range abuse remains a viable option. Between 3 metres and 1.2 metres is the Social-Consultative Zone, suitable for general conversation as in a bar. Personal Space is scientifically defined as a zone around your body from 0.5 metre to 1.2 metres. This is privacy, while if you are closer to someone that 0.5 metres it will be assumed by him, or her, or by anybody observing you, that you are, have been, or will be soon in a condition of intimacy.

In Personal Space and Intimate Space, eye contact is an essential part of visual language. Too much eye contact suggests a disagreeable tendency to psychological dominance. None at all, or too little, makes you look shifty, furtive or guilty. Moreover, attitudes and moods can be quite precisely calibrated by measuring the dilation of the pupils: there may well be an important pre-intellectual explanation of the fact that the dilated pupils of certain animals and babies are universally found attractive, while science tells us that when we are interested in something, our pupils dilate. Charles Darwin dealt with these matters in his book *The Expression of the Emotions in Man and Animals* (1872).

Personal Space apart, the anthropologist Desmond Morris helpfully defined the twelve steps taken on the way to achieving the ultimate goal of consummate sexual intimacy. In this countdown to courtship, significantly, voice is only involved in one of them. Ninety per cent is non-verbal. From the most distant and innocent of contacts to the most intensely personal, the list reads as follows:

1. **Eye to body**
2. **Eye to eye**
3. **Voice to voice**
4. **Hand to hand**
5. **Arm to shoulder**
6. **Arm to waist**
7. **Mouth to mouth**
8. **Hand to head**
9. **Hand to body**
10. **Mouth to breast**
11. **Hand to genitals**
12. **Genitals to genitals**

While genital-to-genital contact is, perhaps undisputably, the most powerful and unambiguous form of non-verbal communication, facial expressions have more social utility since even in these liberated times genital-to-genital contact is conventionally managed in a private context. The face has more dramatic range than the hands, therefore more ambiguity, although it can be just as directly revealing. Duncan in *Macbeth* says, 'There's no art/To find the mind's construction in the face'. And Jorge Luis Borges very beautifully wrote: 'A man sets himself the task of depicting the world. Year after year, he fills a space with images of provinces, kingdoms, mountains, bays, ships, islands, fishes, rooms, instruments, stars, horses and people. Just before he dies, he discovers that out of this patient labyrinth of lines emerge the features of his own face.'

Paul Ekman and Wallace Friesen developed the Facial Action Coding System (FACS) in 1976. They have catalogued forty-six facial expressions which have now become well understood and established norms in visual language. Such is the clarity of Ekman's and Friesen's catalogue that computers can now be programmed to read – not, it must be admitted, with inevitable accuracy – emotions from the list of blinks, winks, jaw drops, lip puckerings and cheek puffs they described. Significantly, Ekman (b. 1934) argues that basic expressions – anger, contempt, disgust, fear, joy, sadness and surprise – are not, as anthropologists once thought, culturally determined, but seem to be universal and innate.

Of all expressions the smile is the most subtle and complex and therefore the most deadly and useful. Dale Carnegie told the sales forces of America to be confident, polite, curious, emotive, but – most of all – he told them to smile. Its ambivalent range is astonishing. In an heroic act of Dada vandalism Marcel Duchamp inscribed a print of Leonardo's enigmatic La Gioconda with the legend LHOOQ, which, if pronounced in French, sounds like 'she has a hot arse', thus, perhaps, explaining her self-satisfied composure. In Santi di Tito's portrait of Machiavelli in Florence's Palazzo Vecchio the great manipulator smiles terribly. Lord Chesterfield, in one of his many letters to his wayward itinerant son, said smile often, but seldom laugh. Since laughter was involuntary and noisy, it was a sign of vulgarity. The smile, in contrast, is calculated.

George Moore's smile was horribly likened to the appearance of sunshine on putty. And T. S. Eliot caught the occasionally bittersweet effect of the flexing of the zygomatic and maxillofacial muscle groups involved in smiling when he wrote that a 'smile falls heavily among the bric-à-brac'. Smiles can be sexy and suggestive. Raymond Chandler's Philip Marlow said, 'She gave me a smile I could feel in my hip pocket.' Havelock Ellis, pioneer sexologist, explained that the same muscular activity in man that becomes a smile is in monkeys a reliable indicator of imminent sexual tumescence. The mouth has well-understood sexual symbolism. Novelist Richard Condon, thinking of another part of the woman's body, wrote of 'the vertical smile'. It is well understood among anthropologists that red lipstick has explicit sexual suggestions. So powerful is this that cosmetics billionaire Leonard Lauder maintained that in hard economic times the last thing women sacrifice is lipstick.

While smiles most readily suggest happiness and well-being, people also sometimes reflexively smile when anxious. Or there is the rictus smile, from the Latin for gaping mouth: this disagreeable expression suggests shock, horror and falsehood. But pleasure, amusement and a certain suggested superiority are the psychological properties most usually possessed by the accomplished smiler.

Cheerfulness is often rightly construed as a sign of wisdom: Victor Hugo observed that Jesus wept while Voltaire smiled. Smiling is an act of cultivation and the cultivated,

There's no art/ To find the mind's construction in the face.

although brain chemists know it has a very specific neurological template involving identified and numbered cranial nerves. A full-on smile releases a menu gourmand of pleasant chemicals, long-chain endorphins (a contraction of 'endogenous morphine') structurally similar to the opiates. Which is to say smiling can make you high. Even practitioners of the insincere smile may eventually benefit from chemical enhancement of their state of well-being. A smile promotes belief and makes you (and usually others) happy. It suggests confidence and wisdom. But, despite Dale Carnegie, too much smiling has a contrary effect: Alexander Pope warned, 'Eternal smiles his emptiness betray.'

With so much of the vocabulary of non-verbal communication invested in the face, the continuously advancing practice of cosmetic surgery becomes a consideration in life's pitch. Lombroso and Lavater long ago determined the predictable features of criminal types, degenerates and the feeble-minded. You don't like the appearance of your face and what it says? You can now change it. Of course, this is no less disturbing a prospect because it is now so viable. The value of a face and its part in personal identity is buried in the deep structure of human thought. Inuit folklore has a story about a mother stealing a child's face. It becomes compulsive. In his book *Cutting Edge* (2004) Laurence A. Kirwan says that Michael Jackson was so addicted to cosmetic surgery that he was in the habit of getting sedated and having pretend face-lifts or skin-bleaching. In movies, cosmetic surgery is rarely treated positively, but more usually as a disturbing and sinister symbol: John Woo's *Face/Off* (1997) was Hollywood's anticipation of the awestruck global voyeurism that attended news of the world's first face transplant in France in 2006.

Cosmetic surgery is biopsy of behaviour, a mechanical way of changing personal identity. Significantly, the first rhinoplasty, or more vulgarly nose job, was performed by a

Romanian Jew, Dr Jacques Joseph, in Germany in 1898. The procedure was brought to the United States in the thirties by Dr Gustave Aufricht, a Hungarian Jew. It is a vulgar truism that Jews are distinguished, and sometimes preoccupied, by the size and character of their noses. So much so that one New York doctor alone, a Howard Diamond, has performed over fourteen thousand rhinoplasties and Kirwan claims that for rich Jewish kids in New York or North London a rhinoplasty is as essential as a late model BMW 4-series convertible or a 5G smartphone.

But it is not only the Jewish community that is in need of cosmetic assistance. Dr Kirwan, now immune from treason through acquired American nationality, has considered the future King and Queen of England, whose position in national life depends so much on how signs and symbols communicate authority. Camilla, he says, needs upper and lower eyelid blepharoplasty, a brow-lift, a face-lift, a chin implant and a smaller, more feminine nose. All this to be followed by full-face laser resurfacing. However, with his close-set eyes and weak chin, only a full-strength cranio-facial surgeon could correct the aesthetic faults of the Prince of Wales ... in Dr Kirwan's opinion.

> **Tattooing is a sign of degeneration and is only used by criminals or degenerate aristocrats.**

Less radical than surgical procedures, tattooing is an alternative form of body modification which speaks its own visual language. David Beckham is the world's most marketable sportsman and he is covered in tattoos. He told *Vanity Fair* magazine: 'I've always said that if I have a tattoo on my body it will mean something to me.' Beckham uses tattoos as part of his personal pitch to the world. The philosophy of this voluntary mutilation seems to be based in the primitive idea of expressing status through excess, while suggesting kinship with favoured causes. Tattoos have the place in contemporary culture of talismans in ritual magic: they impose a behavioural style on the wearer and at the same time speak a startling language to the observer.

Just as Cesare Lombroso had argued that criminals can be identified by facial types and other physical straits, so there is a very high incidence of tattooing among the criminal classes, who regard them as a sort of service record, badges of dishonour. Lombroso's helpful idea became discredited when taken up with a little too much enthusiasm by Max Nordau, whose book *Degeneration* (1892) was a significant source of Nazi theory. Nordau explained that a decadent society 'produces too great a number of individuals unfit for the labour of common life'.

But it was not only mad scientists who believed in a ruinous link between body modification, decoration and piercing, and recidivism. In 1908 the distinguished Viennese architect Adolf Loos wrote an essay called 'Ornament und Verbrechen'. His argument was that since any form of decoration was subject to the tides of taste it would inevitably go out of date, rendering any decorated object or body wastefully useless. 'The Papuan', he wrote, 'covers everything in his reach with decoration . . . But today tattooing is a sign of degeneration and is only used by criminals or degenerate aristocrats.'

The presence of a tattoo betrays not a daring independence, a need to pitch individualism, but a pitiable need to conform. Most revealing in this respect is Japan, where the link between tattooing and criminality is explicit. Confucian culture with its insistence on filial piety rejected the idea of mutilation as disrespectful. In addition, they despised the aboriginal Hairy Ainu who favoured facial tattoos. Accordingly, to the fastidious Japanese tattoos have potently negative associations. So much so that in 1720 tattooing was instituted as a punishment for criminals, replacing the hitherto customary and much messier tradition of amputating noses and ears.

One may smile, and smile, and be a villain.

Given such indisputable and unambiguous stigmata, Japanese criminals became visible outcasts. Known originally as *ronin*, they evolved into *yakuza*, Japan's professional criminal class. Penal tattooing was removed from the statute books in 1870, but a taste for full body art remained. And today, in an almost touching gesture of social promotion, many yakuza insist on elaborate tattoos that at once ape the armour of the old samurai while expressing kinship with the community of thieves. The yakuza taste for voluntary mutilation also extends to amputation of a finger joint as a rite of passage, but significantly there have been recent reports from Tokyo of the more sophisticated Japanese criminals seeking remedial surgery for restoration of lost digits and the removal of stigmatizing tattoos. The English Marxist historian Eric Hobsbawm once said, 'The less sophisticated the mass public, the greater the appeal of decoration.' And the inverse is true: the more sophisticated the public, the less the appeal of decoration.

Body-modification is self-design of the most fundamental sort. The philosophical basis of all body modifications is the need to express power or the search for beauty. This has concerned artists for longer than it has interested scientists. Indeed, the scientific study of beauty might be said to begin as recently as the middle of the last century with Francis Galton's *Beauty Map of Great Britain.* Galton (1822–1911) was a magnificent eccentric, grandson of Erasmus Darwin and cousin of Charles Darwin. He pioneered accurate fingerprinting, discovered the anticyclone and travelled to Africa with a sextant, which he used to measure the fine curvature of the breasts of native women. With entirely subjective criteria – although bosoms remained a constant – Galton's 3 declared that the finest examples of womanhood were to be found in London, the meanest in Aberdeen.

But the calibration of visual language is now more scientific. Functional MRI is one of the techniques neuro-physiologists at London University's Wellcome Department of Imaging Neuroscience use to determine whether there are identifiable parts of the brain (known as 'neural colonies') which react in predictable ways. It is now known that when experimental subjects considered pictures previously determined to be beautiful, neutral or ugly, the scanner picked up the fact that the orbito-frontal cortex behaved differently with beauty and ugliness. But, as if to prove that the science of visual language is imprecise, or maybe just paradoxical, the brain's motor cortex was more vigorously stimulated by ugliness than beauty! There are neural correlates of beauty and, indeed, of every other expression in visual language. But they are perhaps more a matter of art than science. It was, after all, Hamlet who said, 'One may smile, and smile, and be a villain.'

SUMMARY

VISUAL LANGUAGE

❏ Body language is at least as important as verbal language.

❏ Be more than you seem.

❏ Eye contact and smiling are vital ... but not all the time.

❏ Do not get a tattoo.

11 Organized lying, or, how to deal with truthiness

ARNOLD BENNETT said he did not object to lying, but detested inaccuracy. In the era of fake news, it is a very nice distinction. Lying suggests meaningful artifice, while inaccuracy suggests a less attractive carelessness. It is a useful distinction in any pitch: the poet Jean Cocteau said, 'I am a lie who always tells the truth.'

'Organized lying' was Harold Wilson's irreverent definition of public relations. Our personal pitch is a matter of public relations, a conversation with the rest of the world that began with first impressions. The business of public relations concerns the design and control of messages and its lessons apply to private relations as well. With immense, settled gravity it is fascinating to explain that the modern PR business was funded by Edward Bernays (1891–1995), a nephew of Sigmund Freud, whose own insights into behaviour still, of course, influence our culture, whether in the breach or the observation. Bernays's *Crystallizing Public Opinion* (1923) and *Propaganda* (1928) are communications classics: he managed to explain what had often been thought, but rarely

> **'Organized lying' was Harold Wilson's irreverent definition of public relations.**

before so well said. The connection between psychoanalysis and communications is a disturbing and compelling one. Indeed, Bernays's methods – he arranged for the US edition of *A General Introduction to Psychoanalysis* to be published – helped publicize Freud in the United States. Bernays's definition of PR was 'the engineering of consent'. This is a rather chilling reminder of Stalin's definition of art as 'engineering of the soul' since Bernays coined it in 1947 when Stalin's devilment was already well known. Although ever at the ready with a memorable illustration, Bernays, a Jew, was unafraid to claim in his autobiography that Goebbels used *Crystallizing Public Opinion* in the orchestration of the Nazis' highly effective anti-Semitic campaigns.

Benjamin Sonnenberg, another PR pioneer (who, for example, through adroit placing of favourable articles in the press, created an image of Charles Luckman, Lever Brothers' president, as a superlative salesman, creating a template for future objectives in corporate PR) described a personal psychology he shared with Bernays in Isadore Barmash's book *Always Live Better Than Your Clients* (1983):

> Here is the phenomenon of a young immigrant who, while he willy-nilly is dumped on the eastern seaboard of the United States, through a process of experiences becomes more American than Coca-Cola and assimilates himself to the point of knowing the latest boogie-woogie beat in the propaganda of his times. I could have sold rugs in Stamboul, but I became a ballyhoo artist. I was meant to operate from Baghdad to Trafalgar Square. I brought to America a kind of freshness but assimilated America's Coca-Cola

idiom. It's as though Paderewski became a Joe di Maggio, or Rachmaninoff took to chewing gum on the stage and twirling a lasso, the way Will Rogers did.

Bernays was a brilliant self-publicist, the perfect self-invention, a professor of pitch. He saw himself not as a carpet-salesman or ballyhoo artist, still less a charlatan, but as a social scientist, administering soothing psychoanalysis to disturbed corporations. He understood the forces of argument, about how minds can be won. In *Propaganda* Bernays wrote of popular opinion: 'Those who manipulate this unseen mechanism of society constitute an invisible government which is the true ruling power of our country.'

Public relations as 'synthetic novelty', if not actual lying, was the subject of Daniel Boorstin's great book, *The Image: Or, What Happened to the American Dream* (1962). Here he coined the useful term 'pseudo-events'. Quoting Bernays, Boorstin (who became Librarian of Congress) says that public relations is not a matter of reporting news, but of making it. The pseudo-event is defined as a happening that:

1. Is planned rather than spontaneous.
2. Exists to be reported. The question 'Is it real?' is less significant than 'Is it newsworthy?'
3. Has an ambiguous relationship to reality.
4. Is usually a self-fulfilling prophecy.

Most of the news is pseudo-events – versions of managed inaccuracies. It is irresistible to ask whether a revisionist approach to public relations and its place in commercial life will follow the reappraisal of Freud that has been a feature of intellectual life in recent years.

The culture of lying is not new. 'Without some dissimulation', Chesterfield wrote, 'no business can be carried out at all.' He added, 'Tell half your secret to disguise the rest.' Literature has many apophthegms about the variable nature and fluctuating value of truth and the power of a lie. In 'The Critic as Artist' (1891) Oscar Wilde said, 'A little sincerity is a dangerous thing, and a great deal of it is absolutely fatal.' French intellectual Jean-François Revel (1924–2006) said in his book *La Connaissance Inutile* (*The Flight from Truth*) (1988), 'Normal man only looks for truth when he has been through all the other possibilities.' In adland, there is a saying: 'I know this story's true, I've just made it up.'

> Without some dissimulation, no business can be carried out at all. Tell half your secret to disguise the rest.

In 1990 *The Times Literary Supplement* reported that two Swiss scholars had produced a *Dictionnaire des Mots Inexistants*. The year before, the great critic and novelist Malcolm Bradbury published the life of a make-believe academic, Henri Mensonge, in a volume, to quote from the flap blurb, that contained 'a useless Bibliography and an even more useless Index'. The Swiss work has remained annoyingly elusive (perhaps the authors were non-existent too). But Bradbury's Mensonge has become well known. In his book Bradbury, a formal academic of the highest standing, messes and muddles with criticism and absurdity, with comedy and commentary, with satire and send-up. You do not quite know where you are.

It is an interesting metaphor of our collective predicament in the face of so much organized lying.

Lies take their place in an age of uncertainty. One of the big quests in contemporary life is actually finding the frontier between fact and fiction, between news and opinion, between truth and lies. Detecting lies may not be just a matter of forensic science or logical analysis, it may just be a matter of close observation of behaviour. Albert Mehrabian, the non-verbal communications expert, insisted that liars tended to talk less and to talk more slowly. They made more speech errors and moved more slowly than those given to be truthful.

Both science and nature suggest a statistical, demonstrable, repeatable basis of truth (whereas the beauty of lies may be that they are unrestrained by any direct relationship with observable fact). In Lewis Carroll's *The Hunting of the Snark* the Bellman says, 'What I tell you three times is true.' This was quoted by cybernetic pioneer Norbert Wiener as a basis for computing methodology. But science also contributes to contemporary uncertainty. In our increasingly dematerialized world, we all talk about sixty gigabytes, but have no idea what they might look like. The extension of this absurdity into the world of self-identity and of pitching is that telling the truth, or getting it right, is no longer as important as making it interesting. Whatever it is.

Fact and fiction, truth and lies are now in discourse, all elements in the poetics of disinformation. Politics in the 1990s made 'spin' familiar, first via Clinton's James Carville, then Blair's Peter Mandelson. Their political language was, as Orwell said, 'designed to make lies sound truthful and murder respectable, and to give an appearance of solidity to pure wind'.

The word 'spin' does not appear in Stuart Berg Flexner's lexographic masterpiece *I Hear America Talking* (1976), but was used by Saul Bellow in his 1977 Jefferson lectures where he says, 'Success today is in junk bonds, in hype, in capturing the presidency itself with the aid of spin doctors.'

The political noun phrase comes from baseball coaching where pitchers are taught to put spin on a ball to control its direction. Thus, when adapted to politics and behaviour, the notion of spin is a queasy mediation between authority and deceit. The addendum of the pseudo-scientific 'doctor' is significant since it has the effect of dignifying the disreputable . . . giving an appearance of solidity to pure wind.

That art is not truth is a principle that can be proven widely and has a significant part in modern culture. Again, there are significant literary examples. Lillian Hellman's *Pentimento* (1973) purported to be autobiography, but was shown to have a surprising amount of fictional content. In 2005 James Frey's confessional *A Million Little Pieces* was second only to Harry Potter in the US bestsellers.

What I tell you three times is true

Presented by the publishers as a memoir of recidivism and redemption, it was a sensation. But it became a literary scandal when it was proven that many of Frey's facts were fictions. Presented as a novel, the book would have been less sensational and therefore less interesting and accordingly it would have sold fewer copies and consequently made less money. Frey claimed his fabrications were 'comfortably within the realm of what's appropriate in a memoir'. But fabrications are not always scandalous. William Empson, perhaps Britain's leading literary critic of the twentieth century, had a highly creative attitude to the citation of quotations in his masterpiece *Seven Types of Ambiguity* (1930). A contemporary, describing Empson's athletic, not to say shifty, intelligence, said, 'If he misses with his feet, his tail catches on.'

On Bullshit by Harry G. Frankfurt became a surprise best-seller. Nothing could better demonstrate the structural place of dishonesty in national life than a book on bullshit written by Princeton University's Emeritus Professor of Philosophy.

Frankfurt says a significant personality trait today is that there is often a 'lack of any significant connection between a person's opinions and his apprehensions of reality', a conceit comfortably within range of Machiavelli's field of understanding. What, in other words, is more true? What you want to be true, or what actually is verifiable?

A predecessor of Frankfurt was Max Black, who published *The Prevalence of Humbug* in 1983. Humbug he defined as synonymous with balderdash, claptrap, hokum, drivel, imposture and quackery. So not quite as bad as lying, but a fine testament to the status of deliberate and deceptive misrepresentation in contemporary consciousness.

Whether it was spending so many years in an American university that gave him his views on bullshit Frankfurt does not say, although his account of his subject is

> **We are all capable of believing things which we know to be untrue.**

nicely scholarly: 'The phenomenon itself is so vast and amorphous that no crisp and perspicuous analysis of its concept can avoid being procrustean.' So we will not attempt one here, except to say that there are occasions when being economical with the truth can be a real investment. Dishonesty may not be the best policy, but sometimes it works.

George Orwell said in *1984* (1949), 'We are all capable of believing things which we know to be untrue.' Orwellian predictions became part of statecraft during the second term of President George W. Bush when he appointed a Supreme Court judge because he 'knew her heart', not in the surgical but in the emotional sense. (The same President also had helpmates who chastised news reporters because they worked in a 'reality-based community', a comment offering unwitting insights into Bush's confused version of consciousness.) Bush's wilful absurdities led to television humorist Stephen Colbert popularizing the term 'truthiness', selected by the American Dialect Society as the 2005 'Word of the Year'. The society defined truthiness as 'the quality of stating concepts or facts one wishes or believes to be true, rather than concepts or facts known to be true'. Thus, at its best, truthiness is like religious faith. At its worst, it is closer to a lie.

> Bush's wilful absurdities led to television humorist Stephen Colbert popularizing the term 'truthiness', selected by the American Dialect Society as the 2005 'Word of the Year'

But how does the pseudo-science (or black art) of public relations, with its lies and half-truths, its manipulations and its devices, its economies and its genius for imprecision, cross over into private relations? Machiavelli wrote to his friend Guicciardini: 'I was sitting on the toilet when your message arrived . . . mulling over the absurdities of this world.' The science of managing ideas has moved on from lavatorial contemplation to MRI scanners. While there are cultural and social and presidential variations of accuracy and reality, science is inching towards a definition of truth. At the 2006 Society for Personality and Social Psychology conference in Palm Springs, it was shown that political loyalists, when faced with contradictory remarks, would respond with a systematic bias that was actually visible in the brain.

But in any successful presentation of self, truth is less significant than feelings. The important thing is a persuasive appeal to the emotions and the instincts, with only limited regard for factual evidence. This is not cynical counsel, but simply to advocate imaginative art as being more persuasive than frigid science . . . no matter what evidence MRI scanners throw up.

Many business pitches today rely on computer-generated slideware. Edward G. Tufte of Yale University, a specialist in the graphic design of quantitative information, has excoriated them as intellectually damaging, a lazy convenience, spurious efficiency, the technology of truthiness. PowerPoint and other systems reduce the quality of thinking because the rigid templates limit the scope of verbal and spatial reasoning. We have argued that the problem with PowerPoint is not that it simplifies too much, but not enough. Great ideas should not be imprisoned in tables, charts and spreadsheets. Some truths are too complex and interesting to fit on to computer slideware. As Burke knew, a clear idea is another name for a little idea. Great ideas are complex and interesting, the challenge is how to communicate them. Best ever advice in this context? Simplify, then exaggerate (although this may involve an element of deception).

The conclusion to this book about self-identity, this book about how to pitch yourself at a sometimes credulous, sometimes sceptical world, this book somewhere between Machiavelli and Dale Carnegie, is twofold. First, an observation of Groucho (real name: Julius) Marx: 'The secret of life is honesty and fair-dealing . . . if you can fake that, you've got it made.' Second, a Zen precept

The secret of life is honesty and fair dealing. If you can fake that, you've got it made

that there is nothing true and that anyone claiming to see truth is lying. Or, as fashionable restaurateur Mr Chow put it, 'Whatever is true, opposite truer.'

In a complex world we are continuously designing identities for ourselves. Perhaps it is true that these designs are the only reality that matters: the presentation of ourselves is perhaps the most significant we ever do.

So, how to deal with the essential truths of this book? In the conduct of human affairs, feelings count for more than facts. Ideas are superior to statistics; appearances matter. It's just another way of saying, whichever way you look at it,

life's a pitch . . .

SUMMARY

ORGANIZED LYING

❏ Lies and inaccuracies are not the same thing.

❏ Opinion and reality are not directly linked.

Appendix:
exclusive interviews
with our
panel of
experts

Mephistopheles

(b. Beginning of Time – Still Active)

A N EXECUTIVE assistant to the Devil who first appears in European literature with the 1587 publication of the Faust legend. Dr Faustus makes a deal with the Devil that, in exchange for his soul, he may have twenty-four years of unlimited pleasure and knowledge. Mephistopheles is the agent, negotiator and, eventually, the repo man. Christopher Marlowe's play has him as a cunning tempter, diabolically reasonable.

Goethe's interpretation in a poem was more sneering and leering.

Mephistophelean has come to mean seductive and conniving and . . . destructive.

Q *How did you get that name?*

A Actually, I made it up. I know it sounds unflattering, but I thought of the Greek words meaning 'not loving the light'. A bit of a handful, but people don't forget it. Sometimes people call me Mephisto.

Q *What made you famous?*

A Well, being only the second person banished from Heaven was a start and got me noticed, but my powers of persuasion became legendary. I can sell anything. A tobacco spokesman in the movie *Thank You For Smoking* is even described as a 'yuppie Mephistopheles'.

Q *Where do you live?*

A Everywhere! Where we are is Hell. It has no limits, you know.

Q *What's your philosophy?*

A Pain and pleasure, success and failure shift as they will – it's only action that can make a man.

Q *And your working methods?*

A Simple folk never sense the Devil's presence, not even when his hands are on their throats.

Sun Tzu

(fl. EARLY 4TH CENTURY BC)

A CHINESE GENERAL in the state of Wu, a contemporary of Confucius, Sun Tzu drew up *The Art of War*, the earliest book on military strategy. It was probably written about 400 BC, although some say that Sun Tzu may be a mythical figure and *The Art of War* a synthesis of older, anonymous fragments. Whatever the authorship, Sun Tzu's fundamental precept has passed into the collective consciousness. Here it is.

Q *How do you win a battle?*
A Don't start one. It is best to
win without fighting.

Niccolò Machiavelli
(b. 1469, FLORENCE – d. 1527, FLORENCE)

MACHIAVELLI WAS born into a respected family of Florentine officials and courtiers at the most vivid moment in the city's history. He made various diplomatic missions, meeting the leading political figures of the day and formulating his distinctive world view – cynical to our eyes, but not (perhaps) to his. The conflict of morality and practicality fascinated him, as did the exercise of power and the possibilities of corruption. Of his many works, *The Prince* (1513) is the most important, a subtle masterpiece of self-interest whose popularity over five centuries made the word 'Machiavellian' current in all European languages.

Q *Signor Machiavelli, how aggressive should you be?*
A By not unsettling men, you will reassure them.

Q *Is it OK if I call you Niccolò? What happens when a meeting goes wrong?*
A By unsettling men either through timidity or malice, you are always compelled to keep a knife in hand.

Q *What exactly do we actually mean by Machiavellianism?*
A It is really very simple. If you intend to injure someone, do it all at once, so that the injury, being tasted less, offends less. But if you plan to confer benefits, do so little by little, so that their flavour may last longer.

Q *What is your fundamental belief?*
A *Si guarda al fine,* as we say in Italian. This means the ends justify the means, whatever they may be. Only results count.

Q *Why has your name become so discredited, a byword for cynicism?*
A It's got a lot to do with that Christopher Marlowe who also created Mephistopheles' reputation. The playwright invented a character called Machiavel in *The Jew of Malta* who said: 'I count religion but a childish toy,/And hold there is no sin but ignorance.' *È vero!* Quite so. Christianity positively encourages suffering; I really don't see the point.

Q *What do you think of your clients?*
A Men are ungrateful, fickle, liars and deceivers, they shun danger and are greedy for profit. While you treat them well, they are yours.

Q *Why do you want power?*
A For those without power, there isn't even a dog who will bark in your face. Or as you say, I can't even get arrested in this town. Power brings its own morality. Might is right, or tends to be.

Cesare Borgia
(b. c. 1476, ROME – d. 1507, NAVARRE)

ENERGETIC WARRIOR, enthusiastic poisoner, incestuous lover of his sister Lucrezia, tyrant, despot, statesman, strategist, blotched and ravaged syphilitic, son of Pope Alexander VI and the model for Machiavelli's 'Prince', Borgia was at the height of his powers around 1502 to 1503. In these years he was with Machiavelli in Rome, Imola and Urbino. Machiavelli's *Principe* was composed in 1513 after some years digesting Borgia's scandalous and corrupting achievements. His courage, intelligence, power, strength, cruelty and cunning were, Machiavelli found, inspirational.

Q *What's the basic proposition?*
A If you do not desire me as a friend, you will find me an enemy.

Q *But you have had a troubled life?*
A Yes, my friend Machiavelli attributed my problems to malign fate (my father died when I was at an impressionable age), but I did catch syphilis in 1497.

Q *What are your working methods?*
A You have to be ambitious. I always say there's no enterprise so great that you cannot make it seem small. You must refuse even to recognize the existence of tiredness or danger. And you must move fast. People say of me that I arrive in one place before people realize I have left the last one.

Q *Human resources? What is your policy with your staff?*
A Simple! I make myself popular.

Q *Any recipe tips?*
A The cold northern nations have a horror of venom, preferring boots, fist, bullet and blade, but I find arsenic, antimony, orpiment and aconite make a splendid white poison which, when hidden in a ring (there are examples in the V&A), makes the ultimate negotiating tool.

Giacomo Girolamo Casanova

(b.1725, VENICE – d. 1789, DUCHCOV, CZECH REPUBLIC)

CASANOVA WAS an itinerant adventurer, diplomat, satirist, mathematician, pamphleteer, gambler and essayist, best remembered now as a noble and refined seducer of women. His *Memoirs* (written in French) were only published in an unexpurgated version in 1960. Despite a reputation as an indefatigably resourceful lover, it has been calculated that his conquests were in fact only about ten per cent of those claimed by Sarah Bernhardt, Guy de Maupassant, Ninon de Lenclos and Elvis.

Q *What annoys you most?*
A Monsters who preach repentance and philosophers who treat all pleasures as vanity.

Q *Do you feel at all guilty about being such a philandering heartbreaker?*
A Not at all. Repentance only benefits crimes and pleasures are realities . . . though all too fleeting.

Q *What is the relationship between appearance and reality?*
A Everything in the world that is famous and beautiful, if we rely on the descriptions and drawings of writers and artists, always loses when we examine it up close.

Q *What's the single most important characteristic?*
A It is only necessary to have courage, for strength without self-confidence is useless.

Q *Any regrets? Any appetite for revenge?*
A No, not at all. Hatred, in the course of time, kills the unhappy wretch who delights in nursing it.

Carl von Clausewitz
(**b.** 1780, BURG – **d.** 1831, BRESLAU)

CLAUSEWITZ WAS a Prussian soldier and military philosopher, mixing with the social and intellectual elite of Berlin. A major-general at the age of thirty-eight, he distilled combat experience and adventures in diplomacy into his book *Vom Kriege* (On War, 1832). Clausewitz reorganized the Prussian army, but is best remembered for his insights into strategy which remain relevant today. Some have seen in Clausewitz's elegant refusal of dogma a prediction of modern complexity theory. He has a small part in Tolstoy's *War and Peace*. So far from being a caricature German formalist, Clausewitz believed in the realities of 'fog' and 'friction'.

Q *That famous thing you said. What actually was it in the original?*
A Der Krieg ist nichts als eine Forsetzung des politischen Verkehrs mit Einmischung anderer Mittel. (War is only a continuation of politics by other means.)

Q *You're a Prussian. Tell me, is it important to dominate events?*
A A novice chess-player soon learns it is a good idea to control the centre of the board. This recognition will recur in novel disguises in situations far from the chessboard. It may help to seek the equivalent of the centre of the board in any situation, or to see that the role of the centre has migrated to the flanks, or to realize that there is no board and no singular topology.

Q *How do you actually know when you have won a conflict or a pitch?*
A It's never so easy. Like a horse pulling a load uphill ... the attacked, in spite of his exhaustion, finds it less difficult to go on than to stop. The great majority of generals prefer to stop short of their objective. The ones with high courage and an enterprising spirit often overshoot and fail to attain their purpose.

Q *How would you summarize your views?*
A You cannot reduce strategy to a formula. Chance events, imperfections in execution and the independent will of the opposition – all those factors I call 'friction' – require any effective strategy to evolve according to continuously changing circumstances.

Elbert Hubbard

(**b.** 1856, BLOOMINGTON, ILLINOIS – **d.** 1915, ON
BOARD THE LUSITANIA)

AMERICAN WORK ethic pioneer, much influenced by the
English Arts and Crafts movement. Believing in the
morality and dignity of work, Hubbard established
the Roycroft community in East Aurora, New York, after a
meeting in London with William Morris in 1890. Here a
printing press was established on the lines of Morris's
Kelmscott Press. Amongst its most famous publications was
'A Message to Garcia', often cited by American mid-century
management as a source of inspiration. His nephew L. Ron
Hubbard was the founder of Scientology.

Q *How best to motivate people?*
A Folks who never do any more than they are paid for never get paid more than they do.

Q *Do you need genius to succeed?*
A Genius may have its limitations, but stupidity is not thus handicapped.

Q *How can I get more done?*
A Enthusiasm is the great hill-climber.

Q *Should we fear failure?*
A The greatest mistake you can make in life is to be continually fearing you will make one.

Q *How do I avoid criticism?*
A To avoid criticism do nothing, say nothing, be nothing.

Q *And a summary of your beliefs?*
A I believe in sunshine, fresh air, spinach, applesauce, laughter, buttermilk, babies, bombazine and chiffon, always remembering that the greatest word in the English language is 'sufficiency'. Oh yes, I also believe I shall make other creeds and change this one, or add to it, from time to time as new light may come to me.

Sigmund Freud

(**b.** 1856, PRIBOR, MORAVIA – **d.** 1939, LONDON)

FREUD'S INVESTIGATIONS into human consciousness – at first scientific, later more poetic – contributed ideas to culture that, for good or bad, are probably now ineradicable. His belief in the active 'unconscious', in the primacy of sexual motivation, the symbolism of dreams, in the importance of understanding everything, was sourced in the circumstances of his own middle-class Viennese intelligentsia, but soon found application elsewhere. The famous 'Freudian slip' was described in his book *The Psychopathology of Everyday Life* (1901). Besides launching the ego and the id on to the world stage, he invented the Pleasure Principle, Erogenous Zones and the Oedipus Complex.

Q *Do you like people?*
A I have found little that is good about human beings on the whole. In my experience most of them are trash.

Q *What is melancholy?*
A A profoundly painful dejection, cessation of interest in the outside world, loss of the capacity to love, inhibition of all activity and a lowering of the self-regarding feelings to a degree that finds utterance in self-reproaches and self-revilings and culminates in a delusional expectation of punishment.

Q *Are you consistent?*
A To be analytically honest, no. My scientific studies have not made me rational. I had an incestuous interest in my mother, a superstitious belief in numerology, I repeated myself repeatedly when describing the repetition compulsion and I am addicted to cigars.

Q *Are you an optimist?*
A Not really. I am inclined towards demeaning interpretations of human motivation.

Emmeline Pankhurst
(b. 1858, MANCHESTER – d. 1928, LONDON)

THE WOMEN'S rights pioneer and creator of the suffragette movement who was elegant and cultivated rather than the butch troll of recent folk memory, was nonetheless herself the daughter of an early feminist. Brought up in comfortable circumstances, she attended school in Paris before returning to Manchester and marrying a radical lawyer. They were active early members of the Independent Labour Party. In 1903 Emmeline founded the Women's Social and Political Union, whose chief objective was securing the vote. This it did through dramatic direct action, often resulting in imprisonment. In 1917 she joined her yet more radical daughters Sylvia and Christabel in London, living in what is now the Knightsbridge Green Hotel. Sylvia was terminally alienated when Emmeline became a Conservative candidate for an East End constituency.

Her distinguished autobiography, *My Own Story*, was published in 1914. Emmeline died the year British women were given equal voting rights to men (thirty-five years after New Zealand introduced universal suffrage): this vast constitutional change was largely brought about by melodramatic gestures, emotional thuggery, special pleading, blagging, persuasion and seduction.

Q *We had a terribly difficult job selecting women for our panel of experts. Why was this?*
A Sexism dominated history, but as my daughter Sylvia said, 'The inferiority of women is a hideous lie.' We have proved that to everyone's benefit. We had to free half the human race so that they could free the other half. We did it with originality, persistence and bravery.

Q *Do you think bad behaviour can sometimes get good results?*
A Absolutely. You have to make more noise than anybody else. I was perfectly happy to go to prison and had no objection to my daughter Christabel shouting down politicians, although I did later object to her strident advocacy of arson. And, say what you like, but Emily Davison throwing herself under the King's horse in the 1913 Derby did not go unnoticed.

Q *Did you ever find all of this hunger-striking and periods in jail a tad embarrassing?*
A We all believed that the moments of greatest humiliation were also the moments when the spirit was proudest.

Q *Your media campaign was brilliant. What were the guiding principles?*
A The Suffragettes made lots of dramatic public gestures, but our policy was based on two principles: 1 Never lose your temper with the press. 2 Deeds, not words.

Q *What was the role of malice in the women's movement?*
A The argument of the broken pane of glass is the most valuable argument in politics.

Q *And your ultimate guiding principle?*
A Well, I have two. The most important is: Trust in God, She will provide, but I am also terribly keen on being continuously rebellious. I find it gets results.

Dale Carnegie
(b. 1888, Maryville, Missouri – d. 1955, Forest Hills, New York)

CARNEGIE WAS a salesman who started running business courses in 1912. His subject was simple: he taught people to be a success. This made him a success. Only five thousand copies of the first edition of *How To Win Friends and Influence People* (1936) were originally printed. The year after, it began selling in its millions. Carnegie's research included reading over a hundred biographies of Theodore Roosevelt. He was unconvinced by science and believed that even in hard, technological subjects the majority of successes were attributable to unquantifiable, but highly persuasive, human factors.

Q *What's the most difficult thing to do?*
A It's easy to make a million. It's more difficult to put a phrase into the English language.

Q *What's the most difficult thing to do in business?*
A Dealing with people. John D. Rockefeller said it was as purchasable as a skinny latte . . . but he would pay much, much more for it.

Q *What motivates people?*
A People are not logical, they are emotional. Prejudice, pride and vanity are what people care about. Praise directly and criticize indirectly.

Q *How do you get people to do things?*
A Make them want to! Get them saying yes.

Q *What's the single characteristic that all successful people share?*
A The ability to motivate others!

Q *Are you argumentative?*
A The only way to get the best of an argument is to avoid it.

Q *Honestly, Dale, reading your book made me feel sick with all that sentimental homespun stuff about blackberry thickets, drinking lemonade on the porch, cute pets.*
A Never criticize other people!

Jeff Koons
(b. 1955, YORK, PA)

A MASTER OF high-concept crapola, Koons apparently thinks he is Michelangelo. This may be a resurrection of childhood memories of reportedly copying old masters to promote his father's business. To pay his way through school, Koons worked on the Membership Desk of New York's MoMA where he dyed his hair red and grew a moustache in tribute to his hero, Salvador Dali. Andre Breton explained that the Surrealist's name was an anagram of 'avida dollars' and apparently Koons possessed a similar lust for money.

After a short period as a Wall Street trader, he soon understood his avocation to make money was better realized in the world of art. By few people's estimate an artist of any merit, Koons has instead played very profitably with the idea of what it is to be an artist today. In this he is assisted by about one hundred studio helpmeets who work on his balloon animals. He is perhaps the highest grossing living artist. Robert Hughes said of him: 'Koons really does think he's Michelangelo . . . the significant thing is there are collectors, especially in America, who believe it'.

Q *By some measures, those understood in Wall Street, you are the most successful artist ever. How did this happen?*
A I had a dream about Louis XIV. He spoke to me and said: 'Jeff, I want you to be the new me'. I have perfectly achieved that. Some people think I am influenced by Willy Wonka, but – really – I am Bambi.

Q *Which part of Europe did your family come from, do you know?*
A From Germany.

Q *So they were a German family?*
A Well. We have a lot of Germans in Pennsylvania. They like gazing balls. Mad King Ludwig of Bavaria liked gazing balls. I love gazing balls. They were invented in Venice. I have been to Venice.

Q *Why celebrate banality?*
A It's all about polarities and equilibriums. I connect with the archetypal and profound. I am awe and wonderment. I can talk rubbish and people listen. I validate crapola and they buy. My teeth are beautifully capped.

Q *How much are you worth?*
A Several billion dollars.

Donald Trump

(b. 1946, NEW YORK, NY)

THE 45TH POTUS began his career as a developer of hotels, casinos and golf-courses. Few of these attracted positive comment from architectural critics, although they did succeed in separating a lot of fools from a lot of money. As his real estate career faltered, Trump became a television presenter where his schtick was to fire (in a most rebarbative style) game-show contestants who did not meet his exacting business standards. His victory in the 2016 election left US sophisticates fighting for breath and led to uncontrollable outbursts of spontaneous sobbing and some violent demonstrations. As President, Trump has insisted that Truth is revealed to him alone and has questioned the existence of facts. His unusual hair-style is suspected to be a product of synthetic dye and artificial integration. His interests include professional wrestling.

Q *With no experience of government or even the military, you became 45th POTUS. How did this happen?*
A Because I am very rich. And you are a loser.

Q *Do appearances matter? Some would argue against a comb-over.*
A I've got great, great hair. And I am very rich. Rich is beautiful. Did I mention I've got great, great hair?

Q *The 25th Amendment to the US Constitution allows a President to be removed in the event of mental incapacity. Are you mad?*
A My people tell me I am deranged. They are good, good people. I've got great, great derangement. And I am very rich.

Q *How do you close a pitch?*
A I use my hands. I have great, great, beautiful hands. You grab 'em by the balls and squeeze hard. Real hard.

Q *What is the secret of your success with women?*
A You grab 'em by the pussy. They may jump and squeal, but, really, they like it. And I am very rich. I've got great, great richness. And wait until I show you my launch codes.

Q *Is eloquence important?*
A Um. Yeah.

Q *You've been criticized for being an ignorant vulgarian. What's your response?*
A That so-called intellectual thing is fake. It sucks. Books are for pinkos, Mexicans and wusses. I've read every book in The New York Public Library. It's a great, great library.

Q *Is personal style important ?*
A No-one has better style than me. I have a very high QI. I look great in my Lone Ranger outfit.

Q *And a summary of your beliefs?*
A I am unbelievable. I've got great, great unbelievability. And it's not a lie if you believe it. And I believe everything except facts. I don't do facts. It doesn't matter what you think if you've got a great arse. I've got a great, great arse. My arse is unbelievable. So is my tan. It's fake.

Index

All our thanks

to Flo and to Jac, to Nigel Bennett, to Eddie Bell, Pat Lomax and Paul Moreton, to Charles Allen, Tim Bell and Gerry Robinson, and to everyone at Penguin Random House, particularly Larry Finlay, Doug Young, Patsy Irwin and Helena Gonda.

Not forgetting Donald Trump and David Cameron, who, just in time for this edition, gave us inspiring insights into how to pitch and how not to.

Stephen Bayley
Roger Mavity